THEA

SPIRITUAL MIDWIFE

New Meaning To Life After Death

Jacqueline Thea

Cover art by Su Skjersaa Lukinbeal inspired by iStockphoto # 9995033

Cover design by Karen Anagnost

Interior design by WordPros

Author photo by Images by Jeff Kennedy

Published by Thea Associates, Bend, Oregon

THEA ASSOCIATES

Books may be ordered from local or online booksellers or from the publisher:

www.theaspiritualmidwife.com

WHAT OTHERS ARE SAYING …

"I completely LOVED it! I couldn't put the book down. It's a great set of tales—tales of adventure, tales of healing. And working with the dying or the already dead certainly does lead one to the same place …that same place my hospice work has led me … 'How do I wake up before I die?'"

Barb Shirland, Former Director Clinical Operations, Hospice Hawaii, Honolulu, HI

"In *Thea Spiritual Midwife: New Meaning to Life After Death*, Jacqueline Thea inspires us to trust our souls' profound journey. Using her own experiences and prolific adventures, she guides the reader into the mystery of the sacred feminine, life and death and our immortal souls. She shows how dreams can direct our lives and how we can make peace with ourselves—no matter where we are in the process of self-realization. Through her myriad experiences of helping those who were dying to find acceptance, including her beloved husband, she shows how we can help those around us find serenity, even as we anchor that in ourselves. Finally, Jacqueline shares how we can effectively guide into the light, those who were not able to make peace before they left their bodies."

Joan Heartfield, PhD, Author of Romancing The Beloved, and Director of the Divine Feminine-Awakened Masculine Institute.

"The book is brave, tender, interesting, unique, full of love and compassion, humor and brilliance. I laughed and I cried. The tears were unstoppable. Truly magnificent. The world is waiting for this book …"

Ali Davidson, author—It's Between You and Me

"It is hard to figure where Jacqueline's story ends and my own begins, there are so many concurrent awakenings …some had me wincing with the honesty of remembering our younger selves… others reminding us of Shakespeare's 'all the worlds a stage' at any age, and through out, remembering, we can take ourselves and our illusions of separation as seriously as we choose, but in the end RE-MEMBERING that it is ALWAYS about connection …and all there is …is LOVE!

Rosemary Lazzaari, Healer/priestess & social artist

"Jacqueline Thea has a wonderful story telling gift!"

Caroline Pincus, Associate Publisher, Red Wheel Weiser Books and Conari Press

To Mitch

The Love Affaire goes on—eternally.

THEA is the Greek word for GODDESS.

In 1985, I realized women usually carry their
father or husband's name. I chose the name "Thea"
to claim the essence of The Sacred Feminine.

I believe that all women are goddesses.

FOREWORD

The content of this book left me with a sense that some of my tentative beliefs are supported by a person with greater knowledge than I have in this sort of area. Even more, I have a sense that she has astonishing relevant talent in it that I will probably never have.

In the 1970s Jacqueline visited me soon after returning from a life-changing trip to India. The aggressive businesswoman by day and party girl at night had mutated into a gently soothing presence. Walking to lunch in downtown Los Angeles, strangers on the street literally leaned toward her as we passed. When we stopped to sit in a park, a youngster set on grabbing her purse warned her with mocking leer as he marched toward it. Then he paused to hear that she was saying in a low voice, "Thank you for warning me, that was thoughtful," as she pushed the purse behind her legs where he couldn't reach it without attacking her. He stopped, stuttered "You're welcome" and stumbled away, seeming unable to take his eyes from her. I thought, *my, my...a soft answer really does turn away wrath.*

A few years later Jacque took a job like the one I held in California, chief deputy director of a Federally funded rehabilitation program, but hers was in Micronesia. We decided to try a small experiment in telepathy. Each morning between 7:00 and 8:00 am, my time, we tried to exchange messages, alternating the roles of sender and receiver each day. We tried for several weeks, to no avail.

One day I forgot. When I looked at my watch it was a couple of minutes after 8:00. In a bit of a panic I hollered, "Jacque! I'm sorry! I goofed! I love you!" A few minutes later the phone rang just as my secretary arrived to answer it. It was Jacque. Without preamble she asked, "Did you just tell me you love me?" It turned out that we had miscalculated the time difference between Los Angeles and Micronesia and our prior efforts had missed each other by an hour.

In the early 1980s she called to say she'd had a dream about my mother that didn't make sense in terms of her own life, so she wondered if the dream was meant for me. I doubted the idea because I didn't think that sort of thing happened—until after I heard the dream. It was about a year after my mother died. Jacque dreamed that Mother was lying on my bed and I was cutting up the backside of her dress with sewing shears. I left the room and Mother said to Jacque: "I wish Carolyn wouldn't do that; just because I'm dead doesn't mean I don't want to look nice." I knew immediately what the dream meant. I was in the process of putting together some of Mother's poetry in a little booklet to give to friends and family. I'd had the arrogance to edit a bit here and there and had also made a strategic error. In the one booklet that had already gone out I'd included a poem in which she poked bit of fun at visiting relatives. I learned that her favorite cousin, whose visits she had cherished, felt hurt, thinking he was among the targets of her clever doggerel. I exclaimed to Jacque, "You were right! She wants me to stop undercutting her! She knew I'd just repress it if she tried to communicate directly with me!"

These experiences made me begin to question the non-validated certainty of many scientists that "paranormal" phenomena are rubbish—which no intelligent scientist ought to believe. By the 1990s I had come to believe in almost nothing claimed as facts, but I now believe in even more possibilities that might some day gain support from future, improved research methods. Contemplative science has begun to spread out of monasteries and into psychology laboratories and field research sites. It has already produced a few startling research findings. And it may well continue to produce more of them as more rigorous research methods are developed, and highly trained and experienced researchers are used. This, I think, is likely to include some of the phenomena described by Jacqueline.

Carolyn L. Vash, PhD, psychologist, rehabilitation services director, research director, and author/illustrator.

ACKNOWLEDGMENTS

My heart is full of gratitude and love to all the souls—wherever they are—who shared my journey and offered their help along the way, especially to my husband Mitch who believed in me and listened.

Special thanks to my weekly writing buddies—Lorna Cahall and Marion Davidson—they consistently offered their insights and critique. I see your fingerprints on almost every page. You have understood and honored my process. Others have shared comments and support along the way—the Writing Sojourners, Wendy Howard, Rosemary Lazzari, Georgia Roth, Barbara Shirland, Roberta Nye, Sandra Ingerman, Hank Wesselman, Michael Harner, Allan Botkin, Joan Heartfield, and appreciation to Richard Groves for our conversation.

Kudos to Su Skjersaa Lukinbeal for the art work and more, Karen Anagnost for the design, Jon Remmerde for the editing, Ali Davidson for being my "ally," and for the advice from Sam Horn and the encouragement from Caroline Pincus.

I'm indebted to many longtime friends who have listened to my stories over the years and have added value to my life—Carolyn Vash, Tricia O'Hara, Zane Bruck, Lynn Galle, my soul daughter—Nancy Beckley, and my associate—Belinda Ashenfelter.

I acknowledge all the ancestors, mentors, teachers and guides whose wisdom is reflected in the text and referenced in the Bibliography and Resources sections. A special nod to Hal Stone who launched my spiritual journey and to Jody Rowe Stanley who continues to share her wisdom. My heart honors my many spiritual helpers and the Great Mother Goddess in her many manifestations, particularly as the Black Virgin.

To All My Relations: abundant hugs to my daughter—Candace Gomber Brey, for her ongoing love and companionship, and for "being there" with Mitch on his end of life journey—to my son, Gregg Gomber, who feeds my soul—and to my son, Kevin Gomber, who feeds my body. We're all in this together. May the healing and honoring of the Ancestral Souls bring support and guidance to my grandchildren—Zach, Jeff, Bri and Max. Blessings on each of you as you continue your life journeys. JJ loves you.

TABLE OF CONTENTS

INTRODUCTION

"Mitch," I said to my husband, as we sat in our favorite restaurant on March 4, 2009, "I need your help with my book, there's more to it than guiding troubled souls." Little did I know as we spoke that in two weeks and two days, Mitch would provide a totally unexpected ending.

My story begins on the night of my 41st birthday. On that eventful night, at the peak of my professional career in mental health, I plummeted out of control—from the heights to the depths—a descent that deflated my pretentious lifestyle. That fall from grace opened a door to another reality where I learned to walk between worlds.

At that moment, I already had three grown children and one failed marriage, but this memoir does not include those earlier times. And as important as my children are in my life now, their stories belong to another tale. This memoir weaves the account of my calling as a psychopomp, a guide to departed souls, and the sojourns and many lessons I learned along the way in my late life transformation.

Thea Spiritual Midwife is written in three parts with an epilogue. The prologue opens with an agonizing dream of my Spanish grandmother Rosella in childbirth. She died in 1912 shortly after giving birth to her sixth child and is still trapped between worlds unable to move on. Rosella waits for a future child to be born who can help release her. I discover that this is my legacy—I am that child.

"Preparation," the first section of the book introduces my initial psychopomp encounter to acquaint the reader with this unusual shamanic calling. The next three chapters describe my heritage and history before the story moves on to my fall from grace and the many adventures and misadventures that propelled me around the world, seeking my legacy.

In the next section, "The Journey," the reader follows my path as I learn how to walk between worlds through exploring many different spiritual traditions including shamanism, Egyptian mythology, Tibetan Buddhist beliefs, ancient goddesses and dreamwork. I find several similarities and agreements between these paths.

"Coming Home," the third part, examines the many practices that inspired my own healing and helped my husband through his transition, which brought the legacy home and made it very personal. It astounds me still that the book ends with me guiding my beloved husband through the labyrinthine pathway of his dying and that he later wakes up on the otherside to become *my* guide to the world beyond.

"Without End," the epilogue shares my life during the first year after my husband's transition. I am in gratitude for the gift of Spirit that opened me to the unexpected and infused new meaning into the term "Life after Death," both for the departed and the survivor. Although my ageless spirit still struggles with the reality of my aging body, I find that this old lion can still roar.

PROLOGUE: Grandmother Rosella

In the crypt of the old Catholic Church, lies the mummy-like figure of a pregnant woman—brown and wrinkled, curled in fetal pose. The body begins to move, the legs stretch out. The mid-wife appears and reaches in to pull the babe from the womb, she cuts the cord that parts the mother and child. A cry rings out.

Holding the babe, the midwife turns and walks away. The body spent, the well run dry, the mother's legs withdraw into their fetal pose. She weeps in silence. The tears turn to stone. She rests.

Then once again—the body begins to move, the legs stretch out. The mid-wife appears and reaches in to pull the babe from the womb, she cuts the cord that parts the mother and child. A cry rings out. Holding the babe, the midwife turns and walks away. The body spent, the well run dry, the mother's legs withdraw into their fetal pose. She weeps in silence. The tears turn to stone. She rests.

The scene repeats again and again and again—the body moves, the legs stretch out. The mid-wife appears and reaches in to pull the babe from the womb, she cuts the cord that parts the mother and child. A cry rings out. Holding the babe, the midwife turns and walks away.

In New Mexico's high desert, at the age of thirty-one on the twelfth day of the twelfth month in the year of 1912, Rosella died nine days after the birth of her sixth child.

The young mother died on the very same day that honors Our Lady of Guadalupe, New Mexico's Patron Saint. Each year on this December day, the faithful walk or crawl in pilgrimage to seek Our Lady's favor. On that fateful day, the pilgrims' prayers for healing could not keep death at bay nor could the fireplaces burning piñons ease the cold. Sorrow filled the hacienda where drapes shrouded out the light and no children played.

"Rest in Peace," the mourners murmured, as they laid Rosella in the ground. But while her buried flesh lay wasting, her heart longed for the newborn babe gone from her womb. Her soul refused to leave and lingered, trapped between the worlds. The bell that sounded and announced the birth and the bell that tolled the death mingled as night turned to dawn.

A child will come who walks between the worlds of life and death and guides departed souls. Rosella waits, knowing that in time this child will hear her cry and rescue her restless soul.

I am that child.

Part One

Preparation

Chapter One

Walking Between Worlds

The pungent seaweed and low fog smelled familiar as I walked from the Del Mar Beach parking lot through the meandering complex of bungalows, looking for the Shamanic Workshop in Room 6A. I expected a Native American elder in buckskins if not feathers as I entered a small ordinary conference room with ordinary people—mostly women— who looked like myself. Maybe I made a mistake—no Native American buckskins, no feathers or beads here, just a few drums in an empty room. Feeling strangely disappointed, I had hoped for drama and mystery.

The shaman turned out to be Sandra, a slim, attractive, mid-age Caucasian woman wearing jeans and a cotton blouse. She gathered the dozen of mostly mid-age participants in a circle and made introductions. An Asian woman across from me smiled. Next to me, a man sat on a Navajo rug wearing a cowboy hat and looked grumpy. In the center of the darkened room, Sandra knelt on a small rug, pulled her long brown hair away from her face, and lit a candle. She began by calling in the ancestors and other spiritual helpers to assist us. Whistling and shaking a rattle, Sandra slowly moved around the circle clockwise.

Sitting cross-legged on the floor with my eyes closed, I waited anxiously as the mesmerizing sound of the whistling grew louder. A vibrating bolt shot through me calling *my* spirit and body to attention. Then as the rattle circled my head and the piercing whistle peaked, so did my physical senses. I quivered. The candle flickered. Then the sensation dissipated as the shaman slowly moved on continuing to welcome in the spirits.

"Many ancient cultures believe that when death arrives unexpectedly, violently, or is chosen out of despair," Sandra explained, "the soul may not know that it died and often experiences difficulty in the afterlife journey. It may linger in the middleworld where troubled souls seek to complete unfinished business before moving on." My ears perked up. "A *psychopomp* is a person who guides or conducts departed souls, giving the living a chance to help those on the otherside who need assistance."

"To learn the role of a psychopomp, each of you will take your own shamanic journey into the middleworld." The Asian woman and I exchanged startled glances. The man took off his cowboy hat. "To begin you must find a place in ordinary reality like a cave, or a well, or an old tree stump as a portal between worlds. After arriving in the middleworld, look for someone no longer living, someone who may have experienced a troubled life or a difficult death," Sandra instructed. (This advanced session required that each of the participants had previously taken a basic workshop that introduced Core Shamanism, the near-universal basic methods of the shaman to enter nonordinary reality for problem solving and healing. We all had successfully experienced finding our spirit helpers and power animals that could accompany and help us along the way.)

Sandra led us through several preliminary exercises to prepare us before we began the shamanic journey to the middleworld. Lying flat on my back, I wrapped my long skirt around my legs, placed a scarf over my eyes, and attempted to make myself comfortable on the floor. The sound of the shaman's drum began to penetrate the quiet room.

The beat of the drum—thump, thump, thump—drew my own heartbeat into its rhythm. It entrained, lifted and carried a part of myself on a journey to another world. The sound faded into the background when my brain began to shift into an altered state of consciousness. In my mind's eye, I approached a grotto, dove into a dark pool of water and swam through a crevice in the rocks that opened into another world.

Alert and sensitive, I entered the alien territory. The barren landscape looked desolate and felt dry. Then suddenly, standing directly in front of me a ghost-like emaciated figure appeared—its pale hand reached out to me. The apparition pleaded, "Did they find him?"

I stood transfixed by the hollowed eyes. Then I recognized the figure as Barbara, an old friend from twenty years past. Her brutal murder by a jealous lover had shocked the whole community.

My heart went out to my tormented friend. "Yes, Barbara," I replied. "They found the bastard and threw him in jail. I hope he rots." The miserable figure heaved a sigh and looked genuinely relieved. I stared at Barbara's restless and gaunt spirit. Apparently she had wandered these many years unable to find solace, not knowing if her murder had been avenged and justice served.

The soul of my friend needed help. Instinctively, I raised my hands over the ghost-like apparition and surrounded her with a healing light. Before my astonished eyes, the emaciated figure of my friend transformed. As she released her attachment to the human realm, her anxieties and fears slipped away and she appeared peaceful.

In the distance a light beckoned, I guided Barbara in that direction. The transcended woman thanked me and walked on alone. I watched as Barbara's radiant soul moved toward the light. With tears in my eyes, I whispered—*Safely home, friend.*

How did I know what to do? Where did that come from? I asked myself. Then the old story that my mother told about my Scots-Irish Grandma Mary Jo came to mind. When distraught neighbors needed help with someone dying they came looking for my grandma who had the gift to guide departed souls—a psychopomp. I realized that my grandmother's legacy had drawn me here.

Chapter Two

Grandma Mary Jo

In the dead of night you could see a lantern swinging in the dark and hear the neighbor calling, "Mary Jo, Mary Jo, we need you," as he trudged across the fields to the farmhouse. Her sleepy-eyed children woke up and strained to listen.

"Sakes alive, I'm coming," Mary Jo called back, then murmured, *I know'd a crossin' to be near.* Mary Jo's callused feet moved from the warm feather bed to the cold floor. "Don't fuss," she told George, "I'll be back later and the girls will cook grits." She grabbed her lantern from the nearby table and fumbled with the wick then threw a shawl over her shoulders. And when the porch door slammed the children whispered to each other, "Someone must be dyin', they always come for mama."

Grandma Mary Jo had a gift. She could *walk between worlds* and when their time had come, guide departing souls on their journey—a spiritual midwife. She had the *sight* and could see the life-light flicker then go out before a person died. And, if you looked closely at grandma's hands, you would notice short and stubby thumbs that could almost double as big toes—they genetically passed down on the female side—some people called them *fairy thumbs.* Fairy blood could account for her *sight,* along with her thumbs; fairies do have magical powers.

The fairy thumbs may have come with the Celtic Scots-Irish blood that ran through my grandma's veins. She descended from a roaming band of independent Celts who fought for their survival marching from one country to the next until they finally moved from Scotland's borders to settle into Northern Ireland. It was said about these people that *they had a discontent that kept them pushing—every generation—a little bit farther into the wild unknown.* In the 1800s many of them found their way to a newly forming United States. These Scots-Irish immigrants didn't fit with the other settlers in the Northeast towns or along the Southern coast, so they just kept roaming, eventually settling into the rugged mountain wilderness along the Appalachians. Later people called them *Hillbillies.*

Those Scots-Irish farmers—those hardworking bible thumping plain folk—loved to tell tall tales. My Uncle Garmon and Uncle Jim told of a time when they went fishing and forgot the bait, but of course remembered their *moonshine.* When they saw a snake with a frog in its mouth they took the frog for bait and poured some *moonshine* down the snake's empty throat and went on their way to fish. Later, and they swore it for truth, the snake came up and tapped them on the shoulder and offered them another frog.

Those Scots-Irish men enjoyed a good fight and avenged all wrongs—real or imagined (think Hatfields and McCoys). They built their stills, held dear their *moonshine* and ran off any revenuers—who took their lives in their hands—if they dared venture into those hollows.

It was early 1900s, in the hills of Tennessee, that my grandma, then a young black-haired lass, caught the eye of a redheaded lad named George. George flirted with the rather plain young Mary Jo and got her pregnant—her folks stood by with a shotgun to insure the wedding. George had always fancied another prettier girl and after his marriage continued to flirt and play the field and often went out on Saturday night and left Mary Jo at home.

George's Scots-Irish great-great grandpa, an Indian scout, also captured the heart of a lovely Cherokee Indian maid and got her pregnant. This affair enraged her Native American tribe and the young couple, fearing for their lives, fled across the ridges of the Kentucky Mountains into Tennessee. After a time twin boys arrived—one dark headed like his Native American mama and the other redheaded like his Scots-Irish daddy, the redheaded one became George's great-grandpa. George's pale skin and freckled face gave nary a hint to his Native American kin.

Mary Jo bore ten children. They all lived except a toddler who died of burns when he got too close to a fire. The surviving four boys and five girls worked hard in the fields, ran barefoot in the dirt, swam in the creek, teased each other, and squirmed in a one-room church on Sundays that doubled for eight grades of school on Mondays. The children slept in the farmhouse attic—the boys in one bed and the girls in another. In the morning, the children fought among themselves for the precious clothes and shoes, giving rise to that old saw—*first up, best dressed.*

Farm life was hard—no indoor plumbing, not even an out-house (Mary Jo birthed her last child in the chicken yard and they nicknamed him *Dommer* after a rooster), no electricity, a wood burning stove, water pulled up from the well, clothes scrubbed on a rub board with hand made soap in water carried from the creek and heated on a wood fire in the yard, milk from the cows later churned into butter, vegetables pulled from the garden, chicken to eat on Sundays after Mary Jo wrung their necks with a single twist of her wrist and picked their feathers clean, (later used for comforters). Mary Jo, George and their nine children lived near the same as all their neighbors—planting, tending and reaping, milking, grazing, and slaughtering, occasionally riding a horse to town for supplies. Life ran with Nature's cycles.

In 1913, my mother Berta arrived—the seventh-born child. Mary Jo called her my *Bert* and, indeed, she was a *beaut.* She came with the fairy thumbs passed from her mother and flaming red hair from her father. She may also have inherited wanderlust from her Scots-Irish ancestor who scouted the Indians because as soon as Bert could manage, about the age of fourteen, she left the farm and headed for the city—first up, best dressed and off she went.

Chapter Three

Little Miss Red Cap

Bert, the young redheaded beauty who became my mother, shook the farm-dust from her feet, ran through the hollows, over the mountains, with a few belongings and found the bus to Cincinnati—where her sister lived and worked—the plot planned for many a moon. Shortly thereafter, Bert found a job and made friends. When those friends proposed to move west, all the way to a place called Los Angeles in Cali-for-ni-a, Bert begged to go with them—stirred by her Scots-Irish blood, wanting to push further into the wild unknown, and she did.

But in this big city, the innocent Little Miss Red Cap met the Big Bad Wolf. At the age of sweet sixteen Bert already attracted men like bees to a honey pot when the panting Wolf appeared at her door. He offered this trusting young farm girl a glittering world of romance, and she bought it hook, line, and sinker. They married. But the glitter soon faded and Little Miss Red Cap wanted out. A newfound friend she met at work named Mame came to the rescue and helped this child-woman get the marriage annulled.

Mame, a Spanish beauty in her own sultry way, took Miss Red Cap under her wing and invited her home to meet her young brother Joe. The dark handsome stranger looked like a Spanish Prince Charming to the young Scots-Irish damsel in distress. She thought herself to be saved. "What strong arms you have," she cooed.

"The better to hold you with my dear," he replied. And another Big Bad Wolf gobbled her up.

Little Miss Red Cap got pregnant. But alas, no nearby parents with a shotgun to help—so Mame arranged an abortion. The farmer's daughter had lost her innocence in the big city, but apparently no lesson was learned because shortly thereafter Miss Red Cap found herself pregnant again. This time the Spanish Wolf in Prince Charming clothing left the maid, ran off to the sea, and joined the Merchant Marines.

The abandoned young damsel dissolved into tears—*afraid, ashamed and alone*. The unwanted seed in her womb swam in the adrenaline's rush that forged the same future feelings—*afraid, ashamed and alone*.

After many months, the Spanish Wolf, with his tail hanging, trotted home from the sea. He married the relieved and very pregnant Miss Red Cap and gave their child a home—although they *did not* live happily ever after.

Little Miss Red Cap never meant to get pregnant, nor did she desire a mother's role. She wasn't unkind or malicious, but in her heart she just wanted to play, to have fun, to look pretty, and be pleasured. And after all, she did have the fairy thumbs and some fairies just want to sing, and dance on tables.

Chapter Four

The Spanish Wolf

Embraced by stark beauty, rugged mountains, and spectacular sunsets, the land of New Mexico shares three distinct cultures living side by side—the indigenous Native Americans, the descendants of the conquering Spaniards, and the Mexicans, a proud combination of the two.

Hidden in the high desert (it is rumored) lives the jackalope. Said to sport long ears like a jackrabbit and the horns of an antelope, it can be spotted at times, usually at night, hopping high over sagebrush or dashing through piñon trees. Although very shy and illusive, if provoked, this *warrior rabbit* will attack with its antlers. Its known fondness for whiskey may be why some people report sightings late at night around campfires—quite often proportional to the amount of alcohol consumed. Other people scoff and say it's just their imagination.

What is not imagination is the innocent blood of indigenous peoples spilt years ago in this high desert land by an invading army of soldiers on horseback. These Conquistadors originally sailed from Spain to the land now called Mexico in 1521. They quickly ravaged the Aztec people, plundered their treasures, and sought to conquer their souls. The Catholic Pope had granted to Spain the right of Spiritual Conquest of indigenous peoples. Queen Isabella and King Ferdinand conferred the right to enslave those conquered.

The soldiers and friars marched north looking for more treasure to plunder, people to conquer and souls to save. In 1598, Juan de Onate forded the Rio Grande and claimed all of the land beyond the river for Spain. He encamped among the Pueblo Indians and founded the town of Santa Fe. In a skirmish, the Indians killed thirteen Spaniards. Onate struck back—slaughtering 800 villagers, enslaving 500 women and children, and amputating the left foot of every native man past age twenty-five.

Indian warrior tribes, such as the Apache, roamed the desert looking for chances to attack the invaders. The Spanish families accompanying the Conquistadors settled the land and lived with a sense of entitlement along with a realistic terror of attack by the native *savages*. Fear ruled their treatment of the peaceful natives they held as servants or slaves. The Christian Spaniards, by the authority of their fierce Catholic God and their Monarchy, determined to break the *heathen's* strong spirit, destroy their culture, and brainwash their children in order to save their souls.

My father Joe—the Wolf in Prince Charming clothing—who finally married Miss Red Cap, carried the blood of those Spanish invaders. His grandfather Jesus, a prosperous rancher, proudly traced his ancestry to the first Spanish settlers. He followed the lead of a Bishop who declared of the natives—"They need to be treated like horses or wild animals. They need to be lorded over and governed by Christians." Jesus regarded his native servants as less than human and often whipped them from horseback as he rode through his ranch. He attempted to live *his* idea of civility in that unforgiving frontier and refused to let his own *purebred* children play with those savage heathens.

Joe's father, Ubaldo Isadore, known as U.I., grew up with that proud sense of entitlement, which seemed to solely extend to the men. In that patriarchal Catholic tradition the women produced offspring, obeyed their spouses, and like children were to be seen and not heard. My Spanish grandfather U.I. married Rosella—a dark-haired, light skinned señorita from a nearby high-desert ranch in New Mexico—about the same time as my Scots-Irish grandfather George married Mary Jo in the hills of Tennessee.

My grandmother Rosella bore six children in nine years and died shortly after the birth of her last child. Being the fourth born and only three years old, my father Joe had no memory of his mother.

U.I. remarried, but after several family misfortunes moved his children out west to the City of Angels. The winsome Joe learned to pick the banjo and charm the girls—including Miss Red Cap, my mother. Following his sense of adventure, he traveled the country and joined the Merchant Marines until his fate brought him back to the pregnant Miss Red Cap, who he had earlier abandoned.

How did an adventurous Scots-Irish carrot top lass from the hills of Tennessee, descended from Celts, find herself in the City of Angels impregnated by my father, a dark handsome Spaniard descended from Conquistadors? I am the child of that fateful mating of mixed origins—not unlike the jackalope—a paradoxical being who united contrasting bloodlines.

Chapter Five

Plunge From The Penthouse

There is a moment in time when, by the grace of the gods, something or someone stops us. We begin with just such a moment in time—July 20, 1973—my 41st birthday.

A year earlier, in 1972, when the "Big 4 0" approached, I questioned whether to celebrate or host a wake. Then Elizabeth Taylor's stunning picture appeared on a magazine cover announcing *Liz Turns 40*! If Liz could turn 40 then so could I. A birthday bash ensued and champagne flowed.

And now another celebration—this time to toast the high point of my career. A unique vocational program that I designed for a mental health center in Long Beach, California caught the eye of the corporate boss. He wanted me to recreate my successful design at centers in San Francisco, San Diego, Phoenix, and Denver. That night at dinner I was to meet the doctors directing those centers. In the morning, I would dazzle them with the specifics of my profit-making rehabilitation plan.

Arriving early at the beach before dinner, I parked my car at a bar to wait for my spouse. Opening the door of my 914 Porsche, I swung my legs around the leather seat, and stood to stretch. Oh, the sports car wasn't the sleeker 911 model, but it was what I could afford—almost new—and the orange color called Vitamin C set it apart. I liked being set apart, feeling special and worked hard for that recognition. My reflection in the window caught my eye. My short auburn hair complemented my appealing attire—a softly draped colorfully striped hand-woven cotton with wide leg pants and an unstructured top had an ethnic flare. Like most of my clothes, never in or out of style, it looked unique and attractive. I wore them with a certain panache. Believing, like Shakespeare, that the world is a stage and we all are players, I dressed for the drama—next act coming up.

It had been a long day. Besides work and preparing for my debut, my mother had surgery for cancer that morning and I awaited the results. It weighed on my mind. But I tried setting it aside, not wanting anything to mar this moment too long in the making. Breathing in cool ocean air, I felt weary, but straightened up, threw back my shoulders and moved ahead—this was my night.

Heads turn as I walked in the bar, but pretending not to notice, I did wonder—*at forty-one, how much longer would they turn?* Age was on my mind—today was my birthday. Sitting down at the bar, I flirted with the bartender, ordered a glass of Chablis, and waited for my spouse.

Ron and I met in 1966; we both worked in vocational rehab when the poverty programs were hot. A tall, slim and fair-haired charmer with a reputation as a known rake, Ron's bad-boy image sent out signals I couldn't resist. We married in Las Vegas the next year. I had just received a master's degree and he later earned his doctorate at USC— we both were late bloomers. Ron grew up in Arkansas, the son of a Southern preacher from whom he'd been running all his life. He was a functioning alcoholic. I had run from a traditional lifestyle with a home in the suburbs and three children. Ron and I considered ourselves cultured swingers, attended nude marathons and enjoyed an open marriage. We laughed and said, "We deserve each other."

I worked and played hard and now I was *movin' on up*—going national. I sipped more wine and wondered again about my mother. Ron arrived and ordered a vodka martini—I had another glass of wine— forgot my mother—it was show time.

We took the elevator to the top of the building. The corporate boss was hosting the dinner in his Santa Monica penthouse. This short balding doctor was quite a local legend in psychiatric circles—a professor, analyst, and astute businessman. His elegant wife, home with a view, stark black and white décor, temperature-controlled wine cellar and all the artifacts reflected his money and style. As the other psychiatrists and their wives mixed and got acquainted over aperitifs, I found—as usual—nothing in common with the typical wives and their conversation of family and food. However, I discovered a Kir cocktail—by simply adding a little crème de cassis to a glass of fine Chablis. *Oh thank you, yes I'll have another.*

I wanted to impress the boss with my new found love of the grape, so recently acquired from a UCLA wine tasting class, but this neophyte got lost as conversation of vintages and vintners rose high above my comfort zone. So I stood toe to toe with the big boys dazzling them with my pitch—the expert of my little corner in their world. "How might I infuse more capital into your program?" I asked. "After all that is the bottom line."

By the time we gathered for the haute cuisine dinner, catered by the famous Chasens, my alcoholmeter registered DANGER. Yet I tried to keep up as the host shared more of his coveted wines. Even before dessert and champagne, my head started to spin. The time had come, while I could still walk, to drive home. The emotions of the day, the alcohol and the excitement of the meeting, all mixed, but did not match, in my brain. And, the next morning I was scheduled to be Queen for a Day, presenting my program to the prestigious doctors.

Facing a 60-mile drive to Huntington Beach, I left early. Since Ron and I came in separate cars, he decided to stay. We'd rendezvous later at home.

Driving down the coast *very carefully* along the San Diego freeway in my fancy car—in my fancy clothes—filled with fancy wine—the new star on the horizon was pulled over.

"May I please see your driver's license," the policeman asked politely.

Chapter Six

Go Directly To Jail

The policeman beamed his flashlight in my face. "You were driving very slowly ma'am. Have you been drinking?"

"Only a little wine sir."

"Would you step out of the car and please walk a line?" Another officer standing by motioned me his way.

"But sir, I have a meeting in the morning and need to get home. I'm not drunk."

"If you refuse to cooperate, I must take you in for a blood test," the policeman's back straightened a little.

I remembered reading a tip for just such an occasion—it suggested you ask for a blood test then stall and hyperventilate. It increased your chances for a lower blood-alcohol level. The officers were very accommodating. After handcuffing me, they placed me in the uncomfortable backseat of their black and white car, and we proceeded to a hospital for the blood test.

Shocked and humiliated, I squirmed in my seat—the handcuffs hurt—they cut into my skin. Then, oh so indignant, I demanded, "Why aren't you out arresting criminals instead of harassing law-abiding citizens like myself? I have to work tomorrow and don't have time for all this. How can you leave my car by the side of the road?"

They didn't pay much attention to me—another babbling drunk.

We arrived at the emergency room of the UCLA Medical Center. I don't remember them taking my blood, the whole procedure didn't seem to compute in my head. I must have hoped the stalling would work and the nightmare would vanish, so I could go home. *Surely I'll pass, I only had a little wine—I'm not a common drunk*, I remembered thinking.

Back in the patrol car and through the darkness of night, the police drove over the hill to the jail substation in the San Fernando Valley.

Of course the police knew this brightly-lit place. Familiar with the routine, they chatted with friends. I felt scared and confused and wondered what came next. The jail, like a Las Vegas gambling hall sans glitter, never shut down. Without clocks it could be any time—all time—no time. For me, time had stopped. After taking my vital statistics, someone rolled my thumb on an inkpad and enrolled me in their underworld cult. I felt like Jonah swallowed by a whale.

The officer then dumped my handbag out on the counter, and picked up a vial of pills. "Do you have a prescription for these?" His eyebrow arched.

"Yes of course, they are prescription diet pills, just to counteract the alcohol so I can keep my balance. Doesn't that make sense?" I replied.

Once out of the handcuffs, a stern, stocky matron took me to a room for a search. Eyeing my fancy clothes, she helped me to strip without comment and then told me to shower. I stood naked in more ways than one. Quickly washing and drying with a small towel, I welcomed the return of my clothes. "I must phone my husband. I need to leave soon," I told the matron. "I have a presentation to make in the morning." Struggling for composure, I took a deep breath and wondered—*Do they know who I am? I'm a star!*

"Over this way, lady, to take your picture." With her large hand the matron took my thin arm and guided my way from the room.

Standing before a camera, I looked up and saw a face in the lens. Is it my face? I stared. A scene from *Lady Sings the Blues* flashed through my mind. Diana Ross playing Billie Holiday is arrested for drug possession and the mug shot shows a horrible distortion of a sophisticated lady. Was there a mirror on the camera or did I imagine *my own* distortion—seeing what I had become? It portrayed a picture of ugliness, evil, and dissipation—exposed.

The matron led me to an empty cell and slid open the metal bars. Dazed, I walked slowly into the cold room and sat on the hard mattress of a steel cot to wait—*ashamed, afraid and alone.* Less than two hours ago, this admired princess held court in an imposing posh penthouse—now I'd turned into a frog. Oh, I know the fairy tale says it's a prince, but *this* frog worked both sides. *Who am I really?* I asked. *Am I the glamorous lady, comparing vintage Bordeaux with my boss in the penthouse? Or just a common drunk locked up in jail?*

My god, I prayed. *What is happening? This can't be real. It's a dream. I'll wake up!*

It was real—my reality—my birthday—1973.

"You can make your call now," the matron appeared at the cell, "only one." She escorted me to the phone.

Oh please be there, I dialed home. *I need you now. You must help me. Please, oh please, be there.* The phone rang several times. "Hello? Oh, I'm so glad you are home. You won't believe what happened. Come and get me. I'm in jail. Please! You're too drunk? It's too far? But don't you understand? Yes, I hear you. You'll call Sam, yes I know he's an alcoholic and has been through all this himself. Yes, I'll wait. He'll bail me out. Yes, I'll see you when I get home. Don't worry, I'm all right. Good night."

"Yes officer, I'm through now. Someone is coming for me. I won't be here long."

"Come this way to the holding cell." Again she took my arm and led me down the hall where several women awaited. They glanced up as I came in to see the new kid on the block. Avoiding their gaze, I moved to a corner and sat down on a cot.

Who are these women? I wondered. *Why are they here?* Some looked like whores with tight and skimpy skirts, revealing tops, and spiked heels, others dressed in leather. *What do they think of me? Am I a whore as well? Of course not, I never get paid. Does that make me better or worse? Oh please don't talk to me. Don't validate the fact I'm here. I won't cry. I'll be strong. I'm all right. I'm always all right. I can take care of myself. I've had to. I didn't do such a good job tonight, but I'll do better.*

Clutching my cloak of separateness—my softly draped colorfully stripped hand-woven cotton with wide leg pants and an unstructured top with an ethnic flare around my body, I waited.

It seemed like forever. I sat, barely breathing, while some women laughed and talked. One bruised woman sat alone and cried. This part of the world I did not know and had only seen in the movies. I didn't belong. *Help someone. I want out. How long will it take? Who can save me?* I'd lost control. Time seemed to stop. I waited. Then shutting down all my senses, I withdrew into my own cocoon.

In the distance I heard my name called. It never sounded so sweet. "Yes, that's me," I replied. "Someone for me?" Thank god. I could leave. "Oh Sam, I'm so glad to see you." Relief swept over me.

"Well, I've stood in your shoes a few times, more than I care to re-member," Sam's Scots-Irish face with faded freckles smiled. "When Ron called, I came right away. I even know some of these guys by name."

"Thank you for coming, I'm sorry to ruin your night. How do I get my car? How can I get home?" I asked.

"Can you drive, are you sober?" Sam looked me straight in the eye.

"Yes, I'm sober. More sober than I've ever been," I answered, return-ing his gaze.

Checking out of the jail, I retrieved my purse and Sam drove me to the towing yard a few miles away—the graveyard for impounded cars.

"You'll need cash to get your car," Sam said. "They don't take checks or credit cards."

"Where do people get cash in the middle of the night?" I panicked. Sam reached in his pocket for his wallet and handed me money.

"You really do know about these things." I gratefully accepted his gift.

His head nodded slowly. "Unfortunately yes."

"Thank you again. I'll pay you back soon." I shuddered, thinking about people whose lives were caught in this dark web. "Good night Sam, we'll get together for a drink soon." I gave him a hug.

It was a long drive home—70 miles. How could I have been so alert? Only four hours before I was drunk enough to be arrested. Where did the alcohol go? Would I dare tell the story in the morning? *Guess what happened to me on my way home?*

Home at last. What a long drive. What a long night. Can it be only five hours ago I left the party? Can a life change so much in that time?

I expected my husband to be waiting. He'd be concerned and re-lieved I was home. He'd wonder what happened and want to hear the whole story. Oh, I wanted him to hold me and tell me all was okay. That's funny—I couldn't ever remember wanting someone just to hold me, really hold me, and brush away my tears. I'd been so independent—taking care of myself—and others. Now I felt different, my loneliness hurt.

Parking the car, I walked up the stairs in silence. *He's not waiting.* Stepping into the dark fetid smell of alcohol, I turned on the lights. He didn't stir—passed out—drunk. How disgusting. I felt disappointed and wanted to cry. *Please wake up and hold me! Do you know how lonely I am? Do you care?*

I *was* alone. No one was there. I had to care for myself and not ask for help. I guess I'd always known—*we are born alone and we die alone and few there are to share the moments in between.*

Shedding my fancy clothes, I looked into the mirror. They *were* the same clothes—it *was* the same house—I drove the same car—but it *was not* the same me—that mug shot embedded itself forever in my brain. Oh God, was I scared.

Chapter Seven

A Broken Doll

*N*o one else noticed that I wasn't me anymore. *Where is my life going? In what direction am I running non-stop?* I asked myself. *What happens in five years—a bigger house, a fancier job, a faster car—faster and faster until I crash again? This time it was jail, next time maybe the morgue. Is that what I want? I must change directions before it's too late. Help! Somebody help me!* Could I say it out loud?

A friend suggested a therapist—a Jungian psychologist. I arrived at his office early for an interview the next week. "Thank you Doctor for seeing me. Last night I dreamt I took a bus to your office and brought along a small girl, but she sat down on the street. Finally, I picked her up and carried her the rest of the way."

"That is called a *presenting dream,*" the therapist smiled. "Sounds like you're ready to work even though your child is resistant. I believe I can help. If you'd like we can set an appointment."

In the first session, I reported *this* dream. "I'm strolling down an empty street in the daytime and see a manhole cover bouncing up and down—something seems to be bubbling out of the sewer."

"Close your eyes and visualize that scene," Hal, the therapist instructed.

"All right, I can see it now."

"Walk over and take off the lid."

"It isn't heavy, it comes right off," I observed. "My god, I see a roaring sewer with garbage floating on top."

"Go down into it," he said.

"You mean just climb down inside? Well, okay, I see a ladder, I'm climbing in. It's not as bad as I thought. It's like an ocean in here."

"What do you see?" He asked.

"I'm underwater. I can swim around." I replied.

"Take your time and explore."

"I see a doll lying on the ocean floor. It's broken and its head twisted. I'll pick it up. Oh, I see a cave. What should I do?" I asked.

"That's enough for today, we'll stop now," Hal instructed me to come back to the surface, then open my eyes.

"It really wasn't too bad down there," I replied. "What did we just do?"

"When you told me the dream of the manhole cover about to erupt, I knew you had stuff close to the surface ready to pop, so I went with it. It's called visual imagery or guided imagination. It's like dreaming only you're awake. We'll explore more on your next visit, our time is up now."

But being an impatient person and unable to wait, the next day at home I started using guided imagery alone. Closing my eyes, I imagined myself back in the sewer cave with the broken doll. I saw a man dancing around with a harpoon in his hand, but he didn't see me. *Oh shit, it looks like the devil!* I gasped. Fascinated, almost in a trance, I moved closer. He looked up and I thought he would hurt me. Grabbing the doll from my hands, he thrust his spear through its chest, but I died. I watched as he rose through the water with my body in his arms and laid it down on the dock.

Next, as it can happen in dreams, my body laid in a coffin at a funeral. Playing the undertaker, the devil acted ever so solicitous to my family and friends. "I'm so sorry, she was such a good person. What a pity, yes, so young, but accidents do happen," he continued to speak as people paused by the casket.

"What a farce! What hypocrisy!" I attempted to yell. "He killed me! Don't let him get away with it!" The funeral ended.

My eyes flew open, afraid to move my heart pounded in panic. *Oh my god, the devil just killed me. What will happen now? Does this mean I'll die? Call Hal, he'll know what to do.*

When I dialed his office, the answering service replied. "The Doctor's not available at the moment. Would you care to leave a message?"

"Yes, tell him to please return my call when he gets a chance. Thank you."

Out of breath I sat back down on the couch. *Why isn't he there when I need him? I'm afraid I will die alone.* Then I sensed an evil presence around me and felt scared. *Get busy. Do the wash. Do something. Don't just sit there,* I thought. But feeling vulnerable, I could not move and dared not leave the house. If something happened, it would look like an accident, but I knew better. *Maybe I should go upstairs and lie down. There is nothing to be afraid of—it is only my imagination,* I insisted. *After all, what could happen in broad daylight?*

I crept up the stairs and stood at my bedroom door, the cat lay dozing on the bed. Suddenly, she leapt up—her back arched with her hair standing on end—her piercing eyes stared.

"Don't be afraid, Pet. It's only me." Then I turned and looked into the mirror and saw an image of the devil. My legs crumbled; I sat on the stair. The cat ran away.

What can I do? How do I protect myself against myself? I wondered. *I can't call the police. What would I say? There's a devil in my house and he's trying to kill me?* Having worked in mental hospitals, I knew this story sounded more bizarre than most. Was I crazy? Had I lost touch with reality? I couldn't call anyone. I couldn't ask for help, they'd lock me up. Wanting to crawl in a corner and hide, I shuddered and waited.

Finally Hal called. "The devil killed me," my voice shook.

"Of course part of you killed another part. It's been happening all of your life," he said. "What's new is that now you can see it. Don't do visualizations again by yourself; you're not ready. Why didn't you tell the answering service this was an emergency and insist on talking to me right away?" Raising his voice he continued, "You must learn to demand help when you need it. Come in tomorrow."

In his office the next day, I squirmed in my seat rather sheepishly, but felt safe. "This time I want you to go back into the ocean," he said, "but I'll be here to help you."

Closing my eyes, I relaxed. "I'm in the cave," I reported. "I see the doll on the floor where it fell when we struggled, I'm picking it up. Its little arm and the head are almost torn off and it's naked." Holding it in my hand, I managed to swim out of the cave and up to the light. Putting the mangled doll on the pier, I lifted myself out of the water. When I picked up the doll, it came to life—I held a live baby in my arms.

Still working as the Rehab Director in Long Beach, I delayed plans to start other centers. The outside search for satisfaction slowed as I began an inner quest.

"Quit using your head," Hal insisted. "Stop thinking. Stop trying to figure everything out. Stop intellectualizing. Stop reasoning. Start feeling. Start using your intuition. Learn to meditate. Quit reading books. You already know what you need."

"But Doctor, how can I learn to meditate if I don't read a book on how to do it?" I replied. "How will I know if I'm doing it right?"

"There are no right or wrong ways," he said. "Just do it."

So the next day early in the morning at home by myself I just sat on the floor, closed my eyes, and let my head clear. Then visualizing a small, peaceful lake with trees all around it, I saw myself sitting in a lotus position by the water's edge and waited. I hoped I was doing it *right*.

My life focused around my weekly therapy sessions with Hal. In another guided imagery session, I saw myself held captive by a witch in the cellar of an orphanage. I escaped—ran through the building and out the front door. To my relief, a cab sat waiting at the curb. I jumped in and the driver sped away. We went faster and faster, my heart raced as well. "Slow down," I pleaded. The speedometer flashed past 100. I pleaded again. Silence. The driver looked straight ahead. "Please stop!" I yelled. Then he grinned, turned his head, and I screamed. I looked into the face of the devil.

"Ask for help," Hal gently directed.

I opened my mouth—nothing came.

"Ask for help," he repeated.

Still nothing would come. The car sped faster.

"Ask for help," Hal repeated again.

Again my mouth opened and this time a hoarse whisper slowly escaped from my throat—"H-e-l-p." Immediately brakes screeched, an angel stood in front of the car with his hands held over his head. Angels sat by my side and another in the front seat of the car. In the next moment, I found myself under a tree in the grass, held safely in the arms of Jesus with angels attending.

Sometime later, just before a therapy appointment, I got a call that a jealous lover had murdered my friend Barbara. At my session I mentioned it to Hal. When I closed my eyes for guided imagery, Barbara appeared. Her body laid in repose then her spirit rose trying to leave and then returned to her body. This happened again and again. Then she reached out to me and yanked my spirit out of my body and together we started to rise.

"Come back, don't leave!" Hal said, when I reported this scene. A tug of war ensued until I willed my spirit back to my body and Barbara went on.

"Are you suicidal?" Hal asked

"No, not that I'm aware of," I replied.

"Your friend's spirit is still unsettled. With such a violent death she may not know yet that she's dead. She recognizes you and is trying to hang on or take you with her. You must stay grounded." He left and got me some food and told me to eat. "I have another appointment, but you can stay here. Don't leave, I'll be back." I stayed several hours in his office until with Hal's help I felt safe. He warned me not to let my spirit leave my body again, without help it might not return. This was my first contact with a departed soul.

Weeks later during a meditation a slight, dark young man wearing loose cotton garb appeared by my side. He motioned for me to follow. We walked from the lake up a hill, over some rocks and to a cave. He pointed for me to go in. Stopping, I stared into the darkness and then stepped carefully inside. In the flickering light of a candle, I saw a man in a light colored robe seated on a rock bench in the shadows. A cowl pulled over his head framed a gentle face with a dark beard and piercing brown eyes. He nodded for me to sit down. "I am your teacher," he said. "I have many things to teach you, then I will lead you to someone else."

I sat transfixed. Was my mind playing tricks? Was I hallucinating? "Give me a sign so I know that you're real," I asked. "How do I know you're not just my imagination?"

"Of course I'm your imagination," he replied, "and you had better pay attention to me."

After studying many months with Hal—my outer teacher—my inner teacher had manifested to guide me. With my daughter married and my two sons out of school and on their own, my soul beckoned me in a new direction. I quit my job, left my husband, sold my Porsche to finance the trip, packed one bag, took a few books and boarded a freighter bound for India on February 21, 1974.

Chapter Eight

All Aboard

No one celebrated my leaving—no *Bon Voyage*. I left my home, my family and friends, my position, the many things I cared for and yet, I still had to let go of the passions that bound me and served me no longer. The "I" that was leaving would not return.

Some friends with fear in their eyes begged me not to leave, they worried for my safety and argued, "Why go all the way to India, can't you stay home and just go on retreat?" My husband accused me of running away. It wasn't running away so much as being drawn away, some unknown force pulling me out of the lifestyle we shared that could drown me. I had to leave, break the suction, or die. No one else understood except my Auntie Mame. When I told her my plans she said, "Good for you! That is exactly what I'd do if I were your age. Good luck." But then the next day she called in a panic. "I had a dream you were in danger. I'm afraid. Please don't go."

"I'm sorry you're worried, but I'll be careful," I promised.

With no well-wishers, not even Auntie Mame, I sat in my stateroom alone. The parties subsided. The visitors left. The ship's whistle blew and the voyage began. Most of the freighter's eleven passengers met on the deck to pay their respects to the Golden Gate Bridge. San Francisco slowly disappeared into the fog.

Later, the few passengers gathered to get acquainted in a large social room on board ship, a place to read, play cards or just relax.

"Who are you? What do you do?" A short balding man asked while popping a shrimp hors d'oeuvre in his mouth, the cocktail sauce dripped on his shirt. I tried not to notice.

A good question. How do I answer? "I'm Jacqueline and I'm unemployed." I settled for a cracker with cheese.

Later in my room, I wrote in my diary: "With my past identity gone, who is left? 'I' still exist—life still has meaning, but where do I find it? To experience myself, by myself, for myself—my loneliness, my pain, and my joy, these are my goals. I want to face the decay and debris I saw in that mug shot in jail. Can I accept the many parts of myself—the devils as well as the angels? In Carlos Castaneda's book *The Teachings of Don Juan,* he says that 'the art of being a warrior is to balance the terror of being human with the wonder of being human.' Am I ready for that?"

Since I didn't play bridge or socialize I read, meditated, walked on the deck, and took long moments just to *be* and journaled my dreams. Time zones changed as we crossed the ocean, and so did I.

One night as I lay in bed drifting off to sleep I witnessed my spirit rise out of my body and hover at the ceiling gazing down at my sleeping self. *What's happening?* I wondered hardly believing my eyes. *Am I dreaming or is this an out-of-body experience? What should I do? I don't feel safe. If my spirit leaves the ship it may never return, and I will be lost.* After Hal's admonition about doing these things alone I knew better than play with visions or dreams. My spirit needed the safety and protection of my body so I coaxed my spirit back down to the bed.

The age of the eleven passengers averaged about 65. As a single woman of 41, the crew glanced my way more than once. From an able-bodied seaman who washed windows to the Captain, who showed me how to navigate by stars, many asked to take me *ashore.*

On our first docking to unload freight in Japan, I walked alone up the pier to the commissary for the sailors. As I approached I saw David, the young engineer. His prematurely gray long hair blew in the wind and his intense brown eyes watched me approach. Dressed neatly in pressed cotton pants and leather jacket, he stood waiting as a young oriental boy shined his shoes. David smiled and asked if I'd like a drink. *What a coincidence that we should meet,* I thought and agreed. Only to find out later that he had stood outside in that early March chill having his shoes shined for over 30 minutes while waiting for me to appear.

David and I flirted as we talked and became better acquainted. "I watched from the deck as you boarded the ship before sailing," he said and grinned shyly. "Then I went to the Purser to get a look at your passport and check you out."

His confession took me back. "Then you know how old I am," I laughed.

"Age doesn't bother me, I feel attracted to you. Do you mind?"

So although he was quite a bit younger, our spirits connected as we talked, and we became friends. Having sailed this same route many times, he shared his favorite places in port.

There are men too gentle to live among wolves, James Kavanaugh noted in a book by that name. Very quickly I recognized that described David. Some sensitive spirits can not handle the pack energy and aggression of life and retreat to a world of their own—quite often through the haze of alcohol or drugs. David had been there, but was now reaching out to connect—to share not only his body, but also his soul. Having already trod this path, he knew the way. Although my husband also had a gentle spirit, the snare of alcohol had proved his undoing.

I realized that David really *saw* the woman who left her old life behind, her emotions still raw from the leaving with an unknown journey ahead. We mirrored each other's dismay with the past, uncertainty of the future, and clung to the moment. In the symbols of dreams—with my body a ship, and my emotions the unsettled sea—David felt like an anchor in a storm.

The freighter sailed for six weeks from San Francisco to Hong Kong— three stops in Japan, two in Korea and one in Taiwan. In Korea I went ashore with a retired English couple named William and Mary, fellow passengers returning home to Hong Kong. We sat on rough wooden boards in a small, motored skiff taking us from the ship into town. At other ports we had found a Seaman's Club that usually had sundries, food and other items for sale. So thinking it safe, we asked directions to the Seaman's Club at that port. A local guide misunderstood and took us to a strange destination.

Upon arrival, we were puzzled and found it much different than the other Seaman's clubs—more like a big house. A large oriental woman opened the door when we knocked and ushered us in. She flashed a smile featuring two sparkling gold teeth, but spoke only to the gentleman, ignoring his wife and myself. In her broken English, and with great pride, she kept saying, "This is *my* house." William, the gray-haired and very proper Englishman could only say "Indeed" as he stared at this bosomy, overly painted woman who showed us *her* house. She asked if we wanted a drink. At the bar several barely clad women sat waiting and focused on William. The light finally dawned on what kind of *house* we had entered. It became clear when we saw the name printed over the door—"Semen's Club." Accidentally, we had been delivered to a brothel.

That night in my journal I wondered—*Was this experience in the brothel a coincidence*? My sojourn in jail with the whores flashed in my mind—the picture of my own distortion—possibly a reminder that although I can run, I cannot hide from myself.

As the ship entered the Hong Kong harbor, I packed my bag ready to deboard. Before parting David serenaded me, "I want to get you on a slow boat to China," he sang and we knew *our* journey had not ended. We'd meet again.

Waving goodbye to the passengers and crew, I watched the ship turn around in the harbor and head for home. Later alone, lying on a cot in the Kowloon YMCA, I momentarily panicked and asked myself— *What in the world am I doing here*? *Did I make a mistake*? The exotic Orient held an unknown mystery yet to be revealed.

My first night at the YMCA a burly, neatly dressed Caucasian man waited for me as I left the café. "I haven't seen you before," he said and introduced himself. "I recently retired as a policeman from South Africa and am returning to England."

"I just got off a ship from San Francisco," I replied, "and on my way to India."

"I've been here before and could show you around Hong Kong," he offered.

"Thank you, how wonderful, I did want to walk down to the harbor and don't know my way." I replied. We walked together, he played the guide and we ended the evening having tea on the roof-top garden café at the hotel. He asked to see me again.

That night I dreamt that I was in a car with this man and we were driving on a lonely road in a rural area, I saw a few hut-like houses set back off the road. He stopped the car and put his arms around me, I felt trapped and started yelling. A few Chinese people came out of their huts, looked our way and went back inside ignoring me. No one offered to help.

Waking up and out of breath, I felt grateful to be safe in my room. My dreams had given me a warning. Was it real or just my imagination? I chose not to ignore the dream and avoided the man thereafter. I had to trust my intuitive senses, they would prove vital on my journey in foreign ports—I counted on my guardian angels to continue their alert.

After a week in Hong Kong, I grew weary of walking the hot streets, the smells of cooking grease, ducks hanging in restaurant windows, the shops and businesses that also housed families and people living on boats in the harbor. I wanted to move on. My ship was leaving for India in three weeks from Singapore.

On a side trip I flew to Bangkok to play tourist before the next leg of my journey. In the Bangkok airport, a taxi driver offered to take me *downtown* cheaper than the bus. But he exhorted a very large fare for a very short ride, left me in a hotel many miles from town and disappeared. Another naive tourist got taken—one of many lessons I had to learn. While visiting a Buddhist sanctuary, a Temple Rubbing caught my eye—the gods of good and evil faced each other ready for battle. I knew well the struggle and purchased the rubbing, rolled it carefully and took it with me as a talisman.

Lying on another cot, in another YMCA—this time in Singapore, I listened to a large wooden fan on the high ceiling make languid swishing sounds as it turned. The constant downpour of rain outside my window reminded me of a scene from Somerset Maugham. Through the long rainy day, I finished reading Hermann Hesse's book, *Narcissus and Goldmund.* The story of two medieval men—Narcissus quietly content with monastic life, while Goldmund searched fervently for worldly salvation.

An inner light flashed. Getting up and staring at the downpour of rain, I began to realize that like Goldmund, unable to find the good mother or love in religion, I sought redemption in my passionate self. As a member of the Baptist church, I had clung to God, religion and reason while struggling with my sensual emotions, seeking to silence the flesh. Then later flinging religion out the window, I sought my womanhood in worldly pursuits—while hoping to silence the spirit. As a Christian, I had tried to kill the Whore and honor only the Madonna. The Whore, denied, sought vengeance. Like a starving wild animal locked away in a cage, she demanded red meat. And, without her the Madonna grew proud, lost her compassion and lifted her skirts to step over the mud—Miss Goody Two Shoes.

Lying on my cot, I wept tears of remorse—tears of release—tears of exhaustion. Writing letters to my three children and their father, earlier victims of my discontent, I sought their forgiveness. Then seeking forgiveness from the Woman denied in myself, the Woman I judged as not worthy, the victim of the inner duel in the slow killing dance in which I took the lead, my tears continued—finally matching and surpassing the downpour outside.

Chapter Nine

India

Another ship transported me to India from Singapore. I awaited a brilliant enlightenment—this *was* India after all.

On a small boat excursion outside of Bombay, I toured a sacred site called Elephanta Island. Our female guide, a psychologist who had to supplement her income, explained the ancient carvings on the cave walls. "Engraved in stone on one side of the entrance Shiva displays the dance of life and death," she pointed with her small hand. "On the other side a priest sits meditating on a lotus flower. Shiva expresses service to the self and to the world; the priest portrays service to his God through prayer and contemplation. Together they represent the balance of life." Adjusting her colorful Sari, she continued, "The Hindus believe in the equal value of both. The attitude with which one does the work makes the difference, not the work itself; all work is deemed holy."

As I stood observing the chiseled images at the entrance to the sacred cave, the guide's words touched me deeply. I thought—*my work is holy. With right attitude, my dance can serve the world and myself and can become my spiritual path, my Sadhana. No need to retreat to a monastery or live my life in a cave. Aha! Now there's a bit of enlightenment. I came to India with an extended visa seeking some kind of truth, a guru, escape, peace, understanding or a different way of life, only to find what I sought outside myself waited unrecognized within. Why couldn't I see that at home?*

The journey continued.

Walking the littered streets of Bombay—the scorching heat, the pungent smells, the invasive beggars, the constant suspicion, the obvious observable pain and resignation kept me on edge. Everywhere grubby children approached me with one hand rubbing their bellies expressing their hunger and the other outstretched for a coin. Cripples cluttered the streets. Warned not to give beggars money or risk being mobbed, I found myself sitting on the Queen's Necklace harbor kicking at children kissing my feet. I shuddered at the overwhelming face of poverty.

Taking the train, I moved north to New Delhi and stayed at another YMCA, but slept fitfully in the sweltering heat. The night before my train was scheduled for Shringar in the Himalayas, my planned destination, I had this dream. *Caught in the mountains, I am in terrible danger and trying to escape. The police come and take me to jail for unknown reasons, I'm locked up and unable to leave.* Startled awake, I lay sweating both from the heat and the fear—the vision felt ominous. Since I paid close attention to my dreams and looked to them for guidance, a warning like that could not be ignored. Immediately I changed my plans, left northern India and flew to Madras in the south hoping to book a ship leaving India.

Arriving late at night, I caught the last cab from the small airport and asked for the YMCA as my lodging of choice. At the cluttered entrance, dozens of sleeping men sprawled on the steps, I panicked and asked the driver to find some other place. He drove to a motel and we argued over an exorbitant fare. After registering, the clerk gave me a key and pointed to a room. I entered and turned on the light. Swarms of cockroaches scrambled, I hardly slept. The next day after changing my residence, I eagerly sought passage on a ship out of Madras. Unsuccessful, I booked the next plane to Singapore scheduled in three days.

As I boarded the plane leaving India, I recalled a palm reader in New Delphi holding my hand predicting I would live to be 87 and visit India again. Shaking the dust from my sandals, and with thoughts of cockroaches and poverty dancing in my head, I swore never to set foot there again.

Arriving at the Singapore airport, I heard my name being paged.

Shocked, I couldn't believe my ears. *No one knows I'm here. How can this be?* I answered the page. A telegram from my husband waited and warned me to be careful; he had dreamt of my danger on the same night as I had my own dream. I had told him of going to Madras and he had a travel agent check all the flights leaving and had my name paged at every arrival in Singapore.

The day after I left India, the headlines screamed that the government had shut down the railroads in a conflict with the unions and had jailed their leaders. Chaos descended—a dangerous place for a single foreign woman traveling alone. The guardian angels had come through again.

Back in Singapore and wondering where to go next, I longed for something familiar—the sounds, smells, foods, clothes, uninterrupted electricity, working phones and toilets, potable water and other things taken for granted. Living out of one suitcase had lost its appeal. As my mind and soul started to heal, my body sought comfort and rest. I flew on to Hong Kong to board another ship and return, but to where?

Serendipity. I couldn't believe my good fortune; life provided small favors. The same ship that brought me to Hong Kong had gone full circle and would now take me back to the States. The crew's familiar faces smiled at me as I boarded and David's grateful eyes filled with tears, they had all worried for my safety. The unceasing strangeness of the past three months slowly faded away.

Chapter Ten

Hawaii

Hawaii—the ship's first United States port, it provided just enough foreign flavor to attract me and had all the amenities of home. Not yet ready for the Mainland, I decided to stay.

Emotionally exhausted, I felt as fragile as a tender new plant. "Oh, please don't misstep and crush me," I said to the world. "I need protection and time to renew and gain strength."

"Hello, is this the YMCA? I'd like a room." I had found the number in a phone booth on the dock. "What you don't take women? Everywhere else they do." My heart skipped a beat. I couldn't afford a hotel. "Oh, okay, do you have their number?" The "YW" welcomed women and had a vacancy. A cab delivered me to my new home. The double room with a shared bath in a warm atmosphere near the University campus included two meals a day at a reasonable price. I settled in.

With my funds nearly gone and unable to face work, I sought help. Hal, my therapist, wrote a note stating because of depression I could not work and unemployment checks kept me afloat.

At Thanksgiving time the staff brightened the lobby of the "Y" attempting to make the transient women feel at home. Although the temperature outside registered 85 degrees, a fireplace provided a different kind of warmth. Holiday decorations adorned the dining tables covered with bright paper cloths for Thanksgiving dinner. The twenty-five or so women that gathered to eat came from many cultures. Although some had not heard of this "American" custom, they nevertheless enjoyed the meal. We all smiled at each other, but had nothing to say.

Surrounded by strangers, joyful memories of preparing past family dinners filled my head. Relatives glad to see each other once a year came bearing gifts of fancy dishes for the occasion. It was always a feast. On this day I waited while others prepared food for the buffet. I put bland gravy on my potatoes, took some dark turkey meat and should have enjoyed the labor free meal. But somehow it seemed the time and effort spent on the cooking added a special flavor. The pumpkin pie needed more spice.

After dinner I walked by myself down the neighborhood streets. Most stores closed on this holiday eve as the merchants gathered at home with their families and friends. I imagined them laughing and arguing like large families do. Feeling my isolation, I looked to buy a bottle of wine to ease the aloneness, but alas, with the liquor stores closed, I found no relief.

That night I sat on my bed, turned on the light, and wrote "November 22, 1974" at the top of my journal—a yellow legal pad. "What is the difference between being alone and feeling lonely? Being alone can be peaceful and is a choice, a conscious decision. I chose to be alone rather than with family or friends when I started out on this spiritual journey. But loneliness can be painful. I do not choose to feel pain. I remember the times that loneliness penetrated my soul like a dense fog even when surrounded by family or friends. Life looked like a cocktail party with endless chatter—so superficial."

Then I felt a comforting presence. "My dear Jacqueline, you are on this spiritual journey by choice not by chance and it is a lonely adventure. Face your fears, and you will find the courage to continue. Your dreams and inner teacher will guide and the guardian angels protect. In your Inner World you are never alone."

That concluded my Thanksgiving Day journal entry.

The days ran into each other then into weeks. I swam every morning before breakfast, walked in the sand, lay at the beach reading or knitting and rode "The Bus" around the Island for 25 cents. The grains in the hourglass sifted slowly—Christmas and then New Year arrived. On New Year's Eve I awoke at midnight in my bed to erupting fireworks on the street (a Hawaiian custom). Shouts of "Happy New Year" rang out. I got up in the dark and shuffled to the bathroom wondering what this year would bring.

On New Year's Day, musings filled my head as I walked on the beach and looked out to sea. As a child, I always helped others. Having a need to be needed and seeking love, I tried hard to please. Being a *good* girl brought praise and pleasure—a compliment from a teacher, a cookie from a neighbor, simple things that gladdened my heart. After High School, I worked as a Nurse's Aide, got married, had three children, studied to become an R.N. and later a counselor, hoping my service to others would fill the deep hole within.

Remembering the cosmic dance of Shiva, expressing the rhythm and harmony of life uniting inner tranquility and outside activity, I wanted to serve my inner self as well as the outside world. There's a Sufi saying—*You can't peel a snake*. At the proper time, the snake sheds its own skin and crawls away, appearing reborn. I saw my life as a series of shed skins—the fates and the gods called the timing. Now after months of not working, I felt ready to try once again.

Shortly thereafter, the University of Hawaii received a grant to provide continuing education to the Vocational Rehab counselors in Hawaii, Guam, and Micronesia—the Trust Territory Islands in the Northern Pacific. They needed a program director and I got the job just in time before the unemployment checks ran out.

Chapter Eleven

Belonging

Accepting the position as program director at the University, my spiritual journey took flight. For two years, I flew to Micronesia and Guam providing education to indigenous counselors, as well as counselors on Oahu and neighboring islands. I flew to the Mainland for training, meetings and vacations—flying symbolized my soaring spirit. But I knew better than to fly too high. Remembering Hal's admonition about connecting my body and spirit, I sought a sense of balance.

I moved from the "Y" and rented a house on Oahu's North Shore. One night a very strange dream puzzled me. *I was at an outdoor gathering of twenty people or so sitting on folding chairs facing a stage in a jungle clearing on the island of Saipan, the capitol of Micronesia. Next to me sat a government official from San Francisco. We listened intently to a slim, Caucasian, older woman on stage giving a talk. When she finished, she looked directly at me, "Welcome to Saipan," she said. I leaned over to the man at my side and whispered, "Do you know who that is?" He whispered back, "Why, that's Amelia Earhart."* I awoke and asked myself, *What was Amelia Earhart doing in my dream and why was she in Saipan?*

The next day at the university library, I searched the stacks for information on Amelia Earhart, the famed aviatrix. Born on July 24, 1897, this courageous American woman had captured the imagination of the world. She disappeared somewhere over the Pacific on July 2, 1937 in an attempt to be the first woman pilot to circle the globe. At the time she was near forty, the woman in my dream looked much older. The mystery deepened. I asked around what others knew about this adventurous woman. A young professor told me, "Oh didn't you know? Some people thought she was a spy. She ran out of gas and went down near Howland Island in the Pacific—somewhere between Australia and Hawaii. There's a rumor that the Japanese captured Earhart and her navigator and held them in a jail in Saipan."

"Saipan?" My breath caught. "No, I didn't know that."

Dreams have many meanings. On one level Amelia represented an adventurous, competitive, pioneer feminist pilot who showed courage in the face of danger. Some thought her ill-fated, a risk-taker or foolhardy. Another story indicated her navigator unreliable and an alcoholic, which said something about Amelia's judgment. Although Amelia had disappeared over forty years ago, the mystery continued.

Since she had found her way into my dreams, her characteristics could symbolize parts of myself. As a dream symbol, Amelia could be both an inspiration and a warning. To me, she slew her dragons of fear and faced her dangers, a pioneer woman who listened to her inner guidance more than outside critics. She became a beacon of hope to a nation in depression. A hero or fool? A tragic figure? Some might think so, but I identified with that woman who trusted her intuition and dreams. I could only hope my journey would not be as ill-fated.

Not long before the dream, I had applied for the job as Vocational Rehab Director in Micronesia, to be stationed in Saipan, but wondered at my chances. Now Amelia Earhart had appeared in my dream and welcomed me there. Some dreams are prophetic. I got the job.

After arriving in Saipan, I asked one of my counselors about the rumors of a Japanese jail on the island. "Yes," he said, "I heard my grandmother tell of an American woman kept there before the war." He drove me to the backside of the island and we trudged through a worn jungle path to the ruins of the old Japanese jail.

The passing years of jungle rot and vandalism had left only the remnants of a cement block of tiny cells in the middle of nowhere. Isolation, like the overgrown foliage, surrounded the cracked and crumbling walls. The roof long gone, rusted pieces of bars that served as doors clung on ancient hinges. A foreboding heaviness still hung in the air. Struggling to imagine the woman's devastation—her dreams dashed—her journey ended in this desolate place—my skin crawled. I remembered the humiliation of my short time in jail. With a burdened heart I called out to the loneliness, "Amelia, were you here? Is this where you died?" A corroded piece of a jail bar that lay next to a tree caught my eye. Thinking Amelia may have touched it, I put it in my car and carried it with me in remembrance. I still have it.

The beat went on. Every month I traveled from Saipan to more than twenty islands covering 3,000 square miles. Visiting the Marshalls, Ponape, Truk, Yap, and Palau, the local people accepted and honored me as a guest in their midst, rather than a foreign official.

Each native counselor I trained had a different culture and speech, but all spoke English as taught in their schools. After World War II, the United Nations assigned the Micronesian territory to the United States in Trust for fifty years and our government programs followed—with varying degrees of success. That is how I arrived. The native culture had been self-sufficient. Born sailors, the men knew how to navigate the seas and were bountiful fishermen. The families grew their own yams, taro root and a few greens. Usually one member of the extended family worked for compensation to purchase other needed supplies. They kept life simple.

As I moved around the islands, the joyful children in extended families caught my attention. The families included the father and mother, the many children, grandparents, uncles and aunts, plus the adults added through marriage; they lived in commune. On a small island, children moved from one family home to another without a sense of ownership, their lives commingled in a natural way—everyone belonged.

When I journaled my observations about extended families, it aroused a deep longing within, an awareness of my own isolation. I wrote: "I began as an unwanted pregnancy and escaped a failed abortion attempt, a place deep inside still feels ashamed, afraid and alone.

My mother and father divorced when I was eight. Once more I felt unwanted. The cycle continued when I divorced, separating my children from their father and friends. I wish I had it in me to belong."

I watched the slow deterioration of these island cultures with our imported TVs, cokes and consumerism ways—it did not bode well. When my contract expired, I chose not to continue working in a program designed to Americanize paradise and decided to leave. I returned to the States to explore my own way of life. How and where became the big question.

Could I still make it in the American business world? I needed one more try. At a conference, I ran into an old friend who offered a job with a national corporation. In the autumn of 1977, I moved to Denver, but traveled extensively.

Inspired by the family community in the island culture, I decided to connect with my Dad. When I was eight he and my mother divorced, and I hardly knew him. We spent little time together and he never showed endearment. I asked him once about his lack of affection. "My mother died when I was three and no one ever loved me," he responded. "I don't know how to love." Did that condemn me to a similar fate?

On New Year's Day 1978, I sought his companionship and we went to the Pasadena Rose Parade together, just us two. Amidst the hundreds of flower floats and marching bands, we enjoyed a marvelous day of talking, sharing and discovering each other. In the evening he made me a pizza—he showed his affection in a way that he knew—his expression of "I love you." I understood and accepted his gift. After the holidays I returned to Denver.

On February 15, my father died. His damaged heart broke.

Days later as I lingered by his casket, I remembered that New Year's day we had shared together just a few weeks before and grieved for past moments lost and for future ones unclaimed—a possible friendship cut short. *What lesson did his life hold?* I asked myself. My father once told me that if you end life with just one friend you are lucky. I'm not sure he did. It was a lonely statement from a lonely man. Was that his inheritance?

As the national director of a back to work program based in Denver, I also had offices in Dallas and Seattle and reported to Rochester, New York. My boss in New York gave me orders and being the middle manager, I passed them on to three program directors. One early December I was told to cut $10,000 from next year's budget in Dallas. The only possible solution was to fire the secretary, a single mother, with two weeks notice—a fine Christmas present. When I called my director in Dallas, he yelled at me over the phone furious that he had to deliver the news to his secretary. I acted tough and said, "Do it!" That night I cried myself to sleep. After two years, I knew the corporate world and I no longer fit. My spiritual growth required a different environment.

Wanting to pursue my interest in spiritual healing, I searched for an alternative college that allowed for the freedom to choose relevant studies. I called old friends, checked different programs and finally found a "University Without Walls." International College boasted over 100 Tutors—internationally known writers, artists, thinkers and musicians—who lived and taught in countries all over the world. They accepted students to learn at the master's feet in a relationship modeled after Socrates. I discovered the college offered a study program in holistic therapy in Los Angeles, which would unite my life's experience and interest. The field of holistic health emphasized the need to understand and treat the whole person—body, mind and spirit.

Earlier in my life, while my children attended school, I studied at college to become a Registered Nurse and sought to heal the body. Later, I studied to be a counselor and sought to heal the mind. On my own inner journey I had sought to heal my spirit, but needed more direction. Now I discovered Hal, the Jungian therapist who six years earlier had started me on my spiritual path, taught as a tutor for the International College. I flew to Los Angeles to discuss becoming his student. We agreed on a two-year program of independent studies, research and writing.

I accepted this training as a gift to myself, helping me to fulfill my soul's quest. My sojourn moved in a new direction. From wanderer to teacher to corporate executive, I now returned to Los Angeles as a student. Another adventure.

Chapter Twelve

Little Sunshine

The University was without walls. Together, my tutor Hal and I created my personal curriculum. It included the required basic areas of study. Two streams ran through Holistic Healing and both shared in common a concern with energy: one stream offered alternative forms of bodywork for healthcare professionals, the other offered psychological process and transformational growth. Research, workshops and other classes would augment my studies over the next two years. I felt ready to start. Hal lived in Los Angeles and I could live anywhere just as long as we met once a week.

I chose to live in Baja, near Rosarito Beach—a little town across the border in Mexico—about a three to four hour drive south of Los Angeles. In Baja, I entered a different physical and mental state; my body relaxed as telephones, television and fast lanes fell behind.

A few years earlier a friend had introduced me to an American community of retirees called *Los Gaviotas*. About 200 houses dotted the hillside and beach including tennis courts and a pool. Some of the residents lived there full time and others came for weekends and vacations. I rented a house and joined the congenial group.

Meanwhile in Los Angeles, I met weekly with a transformational and healing group led by Hal. Several successful business people, who wanted more out of life than money and outward power, sought to access their inner power. The group soon found that it was their vulnerable self—the inner child—that needed attention.

Gregg, the well-dressed mid-age banker admitted that at work he only revealed the part of his self that divided and conquered the world. "That vulnerable child would be crushed in the marketplace," he admitted.

Margot, the sassy insurance broker spoke up, "I agree, but I've found that my inner child likes to play and get hugs. I want to tell you that really feels good. I just have to be careful when and where I let her out." Everyone laughed.

Hal interjected, "Locked away, hidden and often abused, the child can become angry and disruptive, but when invited into consciousness and relationship with others, it can reveal a whole new world."

When at home in Mexico, I walked on the beach at sunrise and watched the changes in tides and the constant surge and flow of the sea. One day a white seal appeared on a rock and stared at me ever so long before we broke eye contact and it slipped away. *Was it real?* Sometimes I found it hard to discern between worlds.

One night on a full moon I woke up crying and wondered why. I rarely cried. Lying in bed I started asking—*What's going on?* Surprised, a voice popped into my head.

"My name is Little Sunshine and I know that sounds odd because most of the time I feel sad, but right now I'm scared."

My inner child had showed up. I stopped crying and listened. Living alone, I often talked to myself, but didn't often answer. "What are you afraid of Little Sunshine?" I tentatively asked.

"I don't want you to move again," she said. "I haven't complained before even though you move a lot."

"Oh, it's about that." I had been considering a move down the coast to a bigger, but more isolated location. "I've only been thinking about it," I said.

"This move seems different," she replied. "I think we might get hurt being so far from people we know. Something warns me that this could be dangerous and I'll be lonely, so I need to speak up."

"I'm glad you did. Why haven't you spoken before?" I remembered what Hal had said. "Were you hiding?"

"I suppose. I don't remember everything, but I know I've been hurt and that I've always been with you." She went on. "Remember the dream you had the night before you started therapy? The little girl who didn't want to go? That was me. And remember the broken doll in the cave and the little girl that broke out of the chains in the cellar and got trapped in the taxi with the devil? That was me, too."

Overtime Little Sunshine began to speak out more. She walked with me on the beach and we learned to play. She told me why she never cried—she had been wounded and hid behind a wall of unshed tears for protection. I wrote this poem for her.

UNSHED TEARS

Frightened little girl where are you?
Inside, hidden from my view,
Hiding, crouching, curled position,
Watching, wondering what is true.

You have been so protected
For lo these many years,
Defenses like bricks have piled and
Built a wall with unshed tears.

Mind was guardian of the fortress,
Feelings had not broken through
Then mind turned round and shattered
And I caught a glimpse of you.

Hurt and scared, eyes that cower—
Wounded bird pushed from the nest—
No comfort and no nurturing offered,
No longer home, no place to rest.

Cry my child, I'm here to comfort,
Sob your tears 'til eyes are dry.
Here are arms to hold your body,
Offering love, a place to lie.

Lift your head and test your wings.
With open heart don't fear to try.
You are a Beloved Being…
Scared no more, you too can fly!

Before Easter I bought three baskets for my grown children in Los Angeles, each filled with goodies and topped with a chocolate bunny (I still did that). Walking on the beach, looking forward to the following day and being with my family, a sad feeling suddenly overwhelmed me. Thinking it was Little Sunshine, I asked, "What's up?"

"No one bought *me* a chocolate bunny!" she replied.

"Of course, I'm sorry I forgot!" She, too, was my child and needed nurturing. I apologized.

We hurried back to the house and ate all three chocolate bunnies. The next day, my other children got a basket of goodies—sans bunnies. No traces of sadness marred our family reunion.

When I treated Little Sunshine, I treated myself. When I loved her, I loved myself—funny about that. As I took care of her, I took care of myself. I liked to buy her ice cream cones and we rode the Merry Go Round at the park.

We grew more comfortable together as we played and became friends. She didn't feel nearly so sad, nor did I. Maybe, just maybe, the real reason I moved to Mexico was to meet my Little Sunshine.

Part Two

The Journey

Chapter One

The Dream

My car radio broke. Long stretches of silent time, waiting at the border and driving to Los Angeles each week for two years became fertile soil for my thoughts.

At home in Baja, the day started early with journalizing my dreams, yoga, a walk on the beach, meditation, breakfast, a Spanish lesson, and then reading—lots of reading, ruminating and writing. What a gift to myself. I learned from so many sources, but dreams came first because dreams came in the silent time of the night and spoke volumes.

I dreamed of caring for a baby—my new life. How I cared for the baby told me how I cared for my new life. I dreamed of food—sustenance—was I hungry? My basic needs met? I shopped in a See's candy store with fudge on sale at half price—delicious possibilities!

I dreamed about clothes or the lack of them—how I looked to the world. Was I naked/exposed, well dressed, or in costume? This revealed how I saw my self and my comfort level with others. Money dreams—an energy exchange—was there enough? Often I looked for my misplaced purse or my wallet—my identification.

When other people appeared in my dreams, I asked, *"Are they themselves or symbols of myself?"* Just before leaving for India, I saw my boss—a psychiatrist—in a dream crying at a bus station. He saw me and fled to the men's room. At our next meeting, I shared the dream.

"Ever since my recent heart attack, I fear dying," he confided. "I feel depressed, but since I'm boss both at work and at home, I can't appear weak or afraid."

Apparently, my unconscious picked up his unspoken fears and revealed them in my dream. He wept as we talked. My dream gave us both a gift because at another level, it expressed an anxiety from my own *inner boss* as I faced a transition in my life.

I kept track of my dreams in my journal and could revisit their messages. Some dreams were prophetic—like the one that revealed my danger in India and the dream of Amelia Earhart welcoming me to Saipan. Some dreams disclosed wisdom, needed changes or warned me of danger—like the dream in Hong Kong of the retired policeman about to molest me. I listened and my dreams served me well.

My adobe casita in Baja boasted a broad view of the sea and a large side garden protected my privacy. I loved to lie on a pile of pillows, read and take notes, then stop and stare out at the horizon and let my thoughts, like the seagulls, soar.

Three books in particular opened new vistas—different ways to perceive my personal horizons. In *Rhythms of Vision,* Lawrence Blair taught me to connect new philosophical insights into the recurring cosmic rhythms and forms, which underlie all life and matter. In *The Silent Pulse,* George Leonard turned me on with his thoughts. "At the heart of each of us, whatever our imperfections, there exists a silent pulse of perfect rhythm, a complex of waveforms and resonance, which is absolutely individual and unique and yet which connects us to everything in the universe."

Writing the ideas of Fritjof Capra in my journal and making comments helped me understand his *Tao of Physics.* In 1975 he wrote that modern physicists have come to conceive the universe as a web of relations and, like Ancient Eastern mystics, recognize that this web is intrinsically dynamic. Matter is not passive and inert but in continuous dancing, vibrating motion—rhythmic patterns. Bells went off in my head when I read "Shiva, the Cosmic Dancer, personified the dynamic universe." I jotted to myself: "Shiva, the figure I saw on Elephanta Island in India. Shiva, who I recognized as part of my spiritual path, Shiva dances the dance of life."

That night in bed, feeling especially alive and in tune with myself, I gently touched my body and caressed her with love. I became the lover *and* the beloved. Then she responded to my touch by contracting and expanding, contracting and expanding in rhythmic patterns. My mind raced with excitement, then relaxed in enjoyment. My senses heightened—the cells, the nerves, the muscles moved in unison, and danced in a rhythm of their own. *The Rhythm? The Silent Pulse of Perfect Rhythm? The Comic Dance of Shiva? Is this it?* I wondered.

For a moment—for eternity—I am at one with all. I am the dance, the dance of creation and destruction, of life and death, the dance of Shiva. Exhilarated and exhausted I fell into a deep sleep and had a dream.

The Dream

It is morning and I'm on the second floor of a large hotel ready to enter a business meeting with several men. I notice drops of blood on the floor and recognize it as my menstrual blood. What a price to pay for being a woman, I thought to myself. Well, considering the options, I'll pay the price. "Start the meeting without me boys, I'll be right back."

I took the elevator to my room on the ninth floor, the top of the hotel. Opening a drawer for a tampon, I am surprised to find pictures from my past that seemed better forgotten—compromising pictures of me with different men. I walk to the bathroom and get on my knees to smear my menstrual blood on the seat of the toilet. Water begins to seep under the door. Standing, I see a giant tidal wave approaching. Being at the top of the building, I worry about my business colleagues trapped below. People are running across the rooftop, I shout at them through the window asking if there's a way out. There is no escape. I remember the hidden pictures then let go of the thought.

The wave crashes over the building carrying me in its wake, its awesome power astounds me. Floating on my back, I watch the hotel walls give way under stress and crumble in the water all around. With only seconds to live, I demand to know the meaning of life. By shear force of will, I hold back the crumbling concrete and refuse to die until I solve the riddle. Then one powerful thought, like the wave, crashes through my mind—it's all about love.

I remember how much I love my children, how precious they are to me. In my mind's eye I can see them—and my mother and father—and my brother. My estranged brother? How bizarre he is here. Yet, I realize, yes, I love even him. In the end, love is all that matters. Death surrounds me and yet I want to live, but I release myself to the flow and find peace in accepting my fate. I am done. I have loved. I close my eyes, and let the crumbling concrete cover me and fade into forgetfulness.

Still dreaming, I wake up in a desert-like setting that resembles the end of a nuclear blast site. A small number of people wander around the desolation with vacant stares looking for someone they know among the few survivors. A woman shows me a pile of containers with food and clothes. We open a box and find fresh-made bread, fruit, and dried grains. "Life is not so bad, someone remembered us," she remarks.

In the distance I see a small group of people sitting around a fire and walk towards them. I hear my daughter telling her story of how she survived the holocaust. She says there are two things she hopes to find—one is her friend and the other is her mother. I'm grateful to be alive.

Opening my eyes, I felt relief—relief to be here in my own bed. I lay quiet, not moving, letting the dream's details settle. The crumbling walls still felt real. Did I die in the dream and wake up in another realm? Was that desolate place a purgatory between worlds? Was I there to help my child? Laying in the darkness I asked myself, *What does this mean?*

Then in my journal I reflected: "The cosmic rhythm that danced through my body in the evening may have set the stage for this epic dream uniting inner tranquility and outer destruction."

The dream began at a business meeting as I competed in a man's world. Then the creative life-giving force unique to the feminine began to flow. Significantly, I moved from the second floor to the ninth—

the top floor. As in a life-review, I was confronted with my past and made atonement with my menstrual blood on the seat of a toilet—a place of letting go. Then, a gigantic wave of water, possibly symbolizing emotion, came over me, but I refused to die until I knew why I had lived. Darkness and death covered the earth, yet I survived and so did my child who represented my inner child. The dream reflected a time of chaos, destruction and rebirth and my own personal resurrection. What a gift.

Chapter Two

Hard Lessons

From school days in paradise to administering a holistic health center in San Diego, I found myself working with like-minded people. It almost felt like finding a family. But after a few months of difficult decisions—budgeting, planning, hiring new staff and balancing alternative health care modalities and personalities—I had to admit the management role no longer fit. Disappointed, I said my good-byes.

A renewed relationship with an aging widower in Baja provided me a safe haven by the sea and a new role—a chance to be cared for the rest of my life. I moved in with Harry, a kindly man who offered me his home, his adoration and his pension. I hoped my feelings could grow into love. Seduced by the easy life-style—not even the backaches, bad dreams, and depression warned me of the weaving web. It seemed to be physical. I had forgotten my holistic training. Naively, I neglected the interplay of body, mind and spirit. I tried to fit into his mold. Harry put me on a pedestal and then grew jealous of those who admired his prize. When a doctor spotted a possible tumor on my ovary, I accepted it as a message of dis-ease. And regretfully, for us both, I said another good-bye.

I acquired a small condo in San Diego near the Jack Murphy stadium and learned to walk on cement instead of sand. Living modestly on the interest of invested money in Mexico—the Peso paid a high interest at the time—I continued to study and write.

Jotting in my journal I noted: "I have a degree in holistic therapy, learned ways to balance body, mind and spirit and yet, my spiritual scales are unevenly tipped. My angels, my inner teacher, my guides all have one thing in common—they speak with a masculine voice. Who speaks for me, for women, for daughters? Where is the Spiritual Feminine point of view?"

In 1982, looking for the Feminine side of God was a little like looking for Alice down the rabbit hole or for Dorothy in the Land of Oz, no one took me seriously. I asked around. My lesbian friends said, "No, I've never heard of a Feminine God, but if you find Her let me know." My Catholic friends said Mary is the mother of God, but certainly not Mother God. Some suggested I check out mythology. My aunt asked, "You mean God has a wife?" Warnings came from well meaning friends not to go off the deep end—not to get so involved with the Feminine God as to forget the *real* God. Having spent over 40 years involved with God the Father, I wasn't worried.

Looking around, I finally found other women searching for the Sacred Feminine. One group met weekly at the YWCA. Sitting on hardback chairs in a cool room we warmed to our subject. "It hurts like hell being treated like a token and not taken seriously," sighed a female minister of Methodist persuasion.

"At least you're ordained," a nun laughed. "I love the Mother Church, but don't like the Fathers' rules. I've stayed and fought for women's rights, but some of my sisters have left and work for equality outside the church. It gets lonely."

"We have problems in our faith as well," a Jewish woman expressed her concern.

"Well, I'm trying to make a difference by helping to clean up the Bible's one-sided language—after all women are a part of *mankind*," a teacher reflected.

A feminist scholar spoke up, "People don't know that God was worshiped as a woman for over 35,000 years until about 5,000 B.C. when the masculine God slowly replaced her, then buried her remnants about 500 AD. The Goddess' demise is greatly exaggerated," she assured us. "Her energy is returning."

The women discussed their religious longings, their sense of being second-class citizens in most churches, and their need to have a spirituality of their own. Many shared, with tears in their eyes, of feeling an unfilled hole in their soul. I agreed—my own soul longed for a spiritual mother. I kept looking

Searching for a tradition that honored a Feminine as well as a Masculine Deity, I remembered that the Native Americans revered the Earth as their Mother. I enrolled in a three-week council in Ojai, California on *The Way of the Shaman* led by Joan Halifax, a teacher of shamanic tradition. This ancient spiritual heritage stretched back into the mist of pre-history—the time of the Goddess—and was now available to non-indigenous people.

For three weeks, a sleeping bag, the hard ground, and a tent became my home. In the early morning, I shivered in an outside shower surrounded by nature. Experiencing ceremonies of the sacred pipe and sweat lodge, prayer offerings and pilgrimages to power places, journeys to visionary worlds, drumming, chanting and sacred dance drew me closer to Mother Earth. Weaving together the teachings of the medicine shields, the myths and stories of the ancestral dreamtime, with ancient techniques for healing of the person and planet, gave me a sample of Native American traditions.

Lying on the grass one afternoon, I looked to the mountain peaks and jotted these thoughts:

> I see the mask of life
>
> I see the mask of death
>
> I am that life
>
> I am that death
>
> It is the Mother Earth I seek
>
> It is the Mother Earth I am
>
> I give my loneness to the Earth
>
> I give my loneness to the Sky
>
> I shed tears for myself/my loneness
>
> I give them away to You/to my Self

Come to Me, my child
Come visit my peaks and valleys
Come to death
Come to life
We are all One
I will fill the empty space.

Early the next day our group of nine people, mostly mid-age and a few younger started a pilgrimage up to the 6,000-foot peak. Not a hiker, I lagged behind with Connie, another slow walker. Then slipping on the clay shale, I rolled several yards scraping the palms of my hands, blood soaked through my jeans at the knees. The scared little child inside emerged, cried a little, then picked herself up, dusted herself off, and hurried to catch up. A couple of hikers in the group sensed my fear and offered to lag behind with Connie and me—the two oldest and bravest pilgrims!

The younger hikers had scampered on leaving our little group to move on the long arduous trek the best we could. The sun beat down— my heart pounded, my throat felt parched, and my legs ached. The quickest way to the top seemed to be through a dry, cracked gully. Climbing over a large rock, I knelt on my bruised knee as John, a fellow hiker, grabbed my hand. The knee wrenched under the weight and a sharp pain caused me to let go and I slipped back. As I clung to the rock, I looked straight down several thousand feet and panicked. My legs shook, my stomach lurched, my mind stopped—I couldn't move. Frightened beyond belief, my world stood still.

After several minutes, which seemed like hours, my legs finally stopped shaking. With a drink of water, my stomach gurgled and I asked what to do next. Mary, another hiker, pushed my butt from behind and John grabbed my arms from above. Together they maneuvered me over the rock. Exhausted, I collapsed and sat for a moment to rest.

We'd lost all sight and sound of the other hikers and didn't know which way to proceed. "Help!" John yelled, hoping someone would hear us and call back directions. A voice echoed from the canyon above, "We're coming." Climbing back down, the would-be rescuers dislodged small rocks that started cascading down the riverbed. We screamed in unison: "Stop!" At that moment a large boulder ricocheted through the gully toward us, bouncing from one bank to another. It almost hit John who sat across from me and then headed my way glancing off a rock at my side. It narrowly missed Mary and Connie and thundered on down the mountain. In silence we listened to it fall, knowing it could have taken any one of us with it.

When he reclaimed his voice, John yelled again, "For God's sake, please stop!" Frightened, Connie wanted to turn back. As John reached over to comfort her, another tumbling boulder cascaded down the mountain and bounced off the rock where he had sat. Speechless, we stared at each other. With no place to hide and with no place to go but up, we all said a prayer and pushed our way to the top. After arriving, I sat down and shook like a rag doll. Then it was time to return.

Carefully walking back down the mountain, I fell behind, but this time didn't hurry to catch up. *I came to this retreat to find the Sacred Mother,* I thought, *but this is not what I had in mind.* Moving slowly, I remembered yesterday's journal entry:

> I see the mask of life
> I see the mask of death
> I am that life
> I am that death…
>
> Come to Me, my child
> Come to death
> Come to life
> We are all One.

"So you want to know the Mother? Here I am—death as well as life. You want to know the Earth? Here I am—the cascading boulder as well as the flowering tree." A voice echoed in my head. "You want to know the Feminine God? Here I am—not all Mother's milk!"

Continuing the deliberate descent, I asked myself. *Do I really want to know Her? Do I really have a choice at this point?* I realized that once you became even a little bit conscious, you could never go back. No matter what the cost I had to continue. Hoping to find a personal nurturing Mother, I had encountered impersonal Nature. She stopped my world. As I pondered the mystery and paradox, my inner child finally spoke up, "Please, can we just go home?"

Chapter Three

The Great Hunger

T his whole mountain climb was damn irresponsible," I accused the leaders who planned the excursion. "I could have been killed!"

"The risk is part of the experience," I was told without apology. "It is a part of the shamanic initiation. You chose to come to this council on 'The Way of the Shaman.' It is not an easy path."

I felt betrayed, but had no response. The shamanic experience was certainly not what I expected. Back home in the ordinary reality of San Diego, I read Joan Halifax's book—*The Wounded Healer*. She described shamans as a type of medicine man or woman especially distinguished by the use of journey to hidden worlds otherwise mainly known through myth, dream and *near-death experiences* (I could identify with that). She focused on the inner journey that shamans take as a part of their initiation and the ways they order chaos and confusion during a life crisis.

The shaman's journey became clearer, but I wondered how it related to a mid-age urban neophyte like myself. Thinking back on the experience, I wrote in my journal: "Yes, I felt called to go on that retreat, and it certainly became a journey to hidden worlds. Yes, I did turn inward to visionary realms and it awakened my imagination. And yes, I definitely experienced chaos and an encounter with death on that mountain, but fortunately I returned in one piece. My three week exposure to shamanism was just that—an exposure. The near-death encounter did not make me a shaman, but it did change my perspective. It plunged me into non-ordinary reality. I saw the face of Life and Death and heard Her voice."

Pondering those thoughts, I realized the shamanic visionary realms were similar to the guided imagery that I experienced with my therapist Hal who set my foot onto this path over ten years ago. I remembered my descent into the sewer, the broken doll, and my encounter with the devil. An invisible connection and continued support led me forward. I must stay the path.

My journal kept track of the detailed events I might otherwise forget. While writing about my shamanic experience, I reread the epic dream from Baja and thought: *That dream could be interpreted as a shamanic initiation of sorts. I was called to a high place and shed my lifeblood. Then my world crumbled. I fell into chaos and death ensued, and my world stopped. An awakening followed, a return with a new focus—the mother and child.*

Starting a new page, I jotted: "Again, the child!" I pondered the implication. *Could she have led me to the shamanic initiation in Ojai looking for the Mother? What would come next?*

As often happens in my life, a book came into my hands that moved me along on my path. Connie, the friend from the harrowing trek on the mountain, recommended the *Mantis Carol*. In this book, Laurens van der Post tells the true tale of Hans Taaibosch, a bushman from Stone Age Africa working the circus circuit in modern America. Hans became an unlikely inspiration who danced his way into my heart.

A typical Bushman with a child-man shape, Hans would rather dance out his deepest gratitude than put it into words. He danced his joy at the birth of a child and his anguish at the death of a friend. For every life experience, he had a dance.

With his head thrown well back and his eyes raised upward with an expression of longing that could bring tears, Hans danced *The Dance of the Great Hunger*. His hands stretched as high as they could, palms wide open, fingertips trembling as if he were pleading, begging, praying to something high up beyond his sight. The name of this great hunger, according to van der Post, was the hunger for love—in the most profound sense of the word.

It's all about love—the same message I received in my Baja dream!

Hans was in touch with the universe and with life in a way I could only imagine. I realized this little man touched me because I shared the same longing, but had no way to express it. I didn't know *how* to open myself so completely, be so vulnerable; I didn't know *how* to abandon myself in the Dance of Great Hunger.

The Bushmen speak personally of the stars and Grandmother Sirius—the brightest star in the heaven. They revered Her as a Goddess and honored Her in religious rite. The Bushmen communed with Nature and depended on Her exclusively. Although taken from his natural habitat, Hans still danced his dance in love, for a way of life lived in love, out of love and for the love of it alone. As a Stone Age mirror, his bond with life spoke to my soul.

I had encountered one side of the Universal Mother on the mountain in the form of the boulder that almost killed me. I had dreamed of a tidal wave and destruction that left a child and her mother separated. I wanted to find this passionate, personal connection with the Earth Mother—this bond with life that Hans knew so well. I longed to dance the Great Hunger that touched my soul.

Chapter Four

The Stream Is Dry

Not knowing where else to start, I went to my local library and looked up the word *Goddess* and started with Greek Mythology and wondered where this expedition would lead?

In the beginning, the Ancient Greeks believed only formless chaos existed, then came Gaia—the Earth. She lived before time began; Time was one of her children. I read that Gaia created the powerful Titan deities who ruled during the legendary Golden Age. But later, a race of younger gods overthrew these Elder Gods. The Olympians supplanted Mother Earth with their own pantheon—Gaia was no longer the primary divinity. She became the ground out of which the later Greek goddesses emerged.

Lounging on my couch in my small condo, surrounded by mythology books, I stared at pictures of the beautiful statues of goddesses who lived on Mount Olympus. They each had their own role or identity—Hera, the wife; Demeter, the mother; Artemis, the hunter; Athena, the warrior; Hestia, the keeper of the hearth, and Aphrodite, the beautiful lover. They did not have the ultimate authority of Gaia, only the male god Zeus demanded supreme worship.

Later, when I read the *Gaia Hypothesis* I discovered the British scientist, James Lovelock, demonstrated that the Earth's systems form an inseparable whole. It functions as a single complex interacting and self-regulating organism. Gaia *is* the Great Mother!

Searching for more information about this first goddess, I read that Gaia had been best known at the foot of Mount Parnassus, the site of ancient Pytho, sacred Delphi. I set my intent to one day visit that hallowed ground.

A few years later in 1987, I went to Delphi to pay homage to Gaia's ancient home that laid claim as the Navel of the Earth. The Great Mother had inspired the holy oracles at Delphi—the place of divine revelation given by prophetic tongues.

My tour guide, named Persephone, explained that the ancients who came with questions purified themselves in the water of Gaia's spring; they called upon Her and swore by Her name. Deep in the cavern shrine, the Pythian priestess, the oracle, spoke of what she heard, answering questions and foretelling the future. In later times, the Olympian gods claimed Delphi for Apollo. Our guide, Persephone explained the many stories told about the takeover—some said Apollo stole the cave by killing the priestess; others said it was given as a gift; still others said he struck dead the serpent Python, child of Gaia, who guarded the oracle's cave.

I asked myself, *What did Apollo, God of Reason and Light, know of the darkness, the womb of the Earth and the intuitive wisdom that came from that place?* "Yet, from the Hellenic times until today," Persephone continued, "it is Apollo's name that is associated with Delphi and the oracle." She looked directly at me, "but Delphi first belonged to Gaia."

Surrounded by dusty sanctuary ruins, I felt the energy from the millions of pilgrims who stood on this sacred earth over the years. Tears moved from my grounded feet up through my body and spilled from my eyes as I listened to our guide read the last oracle uttered by the prophetess in AD 363 when Emperor Julian sent for advice:

"Tell ye the King: the carven hall is fallen in decay;

Apollo hath no chapel left, no prophesying bay,

No talking spring. The stream is dry and had so much to say."

Walking in silence down the hill from this revered place, my heart ached at the loss of the Earth's wisdom. *Yes,* I thought, *the stream is dry. How do we hear the oracle's voice today?*

That evening, back in my hotel, I pulled out my journal: "For centuries man has suppressed the knowledge of Gaia as a living, breathing organism and wantonly used her for his pleasure and profit," I wrote. "But I can't let myself off the hook. I've been slow to recognize and honor her as my life-giving mother. I feel as if my own spring is dry. Please don't let it be too late."

But even back in 1984, as I buried myself in library books, Gaia the Great Mother Earth, and the many Olympian Greek goddesses, felt familiar. I realized that the Great Mother God has many names, many faces, and a different name for each feminine role, but she is One. Just as the many characters in my dream can be a part of myself, when I awaken there is only one dreamer and there is only one Great Mother God.

Chapter Five

The Lost Mother

It is said when the pupil is ready the teacher appears. I remembered in 1972, that a male teacher appeared to me after I learned to meditate. When I asked if he was just my imagination, he replied, "Of course I'm your imagination and you had better pay attention to me." And I did. He also said that eventually he would lead me to another teacher. Now in 1984 my spiritual path had spiraled around to another level and the teachings of the Goddess appeared.

Pondering the idea of one Great Goddess becoming many goddesses, I scoured through the library books gathered around me and found the *Hymn to Demeter*—the Homeric poem about Demeter, the Mother Earth in the Greek pantheon and her daughter Persephone. Written as early as 8th Century BCE, this ancient tale of a loving mother and daughter relationship interested me because in my life, I felt like a motherless child.

My second floor condo faced east and the early morning sun cast dust beams of light on the posts of my brass bed in the loft. I poured myself a cup of tea from a hot pot, propped myself up in bed, and prepared for some personal enlightenment. As I read the unfamiliar poem, the story unfolded.

One day as Persephone played outside in the fields, she bent to smell a narcissus flower. At that moment, the earth opened up and Hades appeared riding a chariot led by black steeds and kidnapped the innocent maid to his underworld kingdom. Demeter heard the echoes of her daughter's cries, but could not find her. After a long and disappointing search, she sat mourning her loss and because Demeter was goddess of agriculture, her depression led to a famine creating havoc on earth. To restore order, the father god Zeus offered to return Persephone, he sent the messenger god Hermes to guide her out of the Underworld and back to her long-suffering mother. During the festivities of homecoming, Demeter despaired when she learned that Persephone had eaten pomegranate seeds in the Underworld and therefore had to return for three months of every year.

The poem recounted the love between the mother and daughter, the pain of separation and the celebration of reunion. It symbolized death and resurrection—the gloom of winter and the joy of spring. Sitting in bed, my tea now cold, *my* heart ached for that mother's love.

Many years later, I had a chance to recreate the drama of Demeter and Persephone's separation in a Beltane ritual on the island of Maui in a workshop honoring the Divine Feminine. Beltane, the ancient Celtic festival of fire, fertility and love at the height of spring, celebrates nature's burst into blossom. With a fresh wreath of woven vines and flowers on my head, I played Demeter, the grieving earth mother. I set the stage and narrated the story of Persephone's abduction. Then, enacting Demeter's shock of loss, a gripping emotion caught me unaware. No longer acting, I *became* the anguished mother reaching out—longing, crying, wanting to hold my daughter in my arms again. My muscles tightened and my heart raced as my trembling hands reached towards the chasm that separated the upper and lower worlds and kept me from my child.

Then across the void, I could hear echoes of Persephone weeping and lamenting the shame of her raped innocence. Stained by the Underworld, she believed herself permanently lost. When the messenger god Hermes appeared to take her home, she cowered in the corner and cried, "I can't leave, no one would want me, I'm dirty. I can never go home again!"

I couldn't believe my ears. I screamed, "NO! That's not true. I love you. I cannot live without you." I wanted so much to touch my child and sooth her hurt and make her wounds go away. But she could not hear my voice across the abyss that separated us. I would have died myself to comfort her, but I had to listen to her argue with Hermes. In my sorrow I could only wait.

How long? How long? It seemed like it took forever for Hermes to convince Persephone of my undying love. Finally, she gave him her hand and he led her through the dark world of Hades back home to my outstretched arms. We collapsed into each other. For those moments, the power of the drama enveloped the actors, as we all stood suspended between worlds.

In the play, I experienced the desperate mother longing for her lost daughter. I experienced the haunting abandonment that consumed the child. I experienced the death and darkness that captures the earth in the depths of winter and the joy of the eternal return of spring.

It took a few days to process the impact of that ritual. Eventually, I could write in my journal: "Reading the story never imparted the emotional force of acting the drama. Now I can see why the Greek Tragedies were so popular, why Shakespeare demands devotees—'The plays the thing.' The world's a stage and the stage thrusts life into the written word. Not only did I feel the anguish of the mother longing for her daughter, but also acting it out allowed me for the first time to hear and identify with the feelings of abandonment expressed from that child and it made my heart ache."

In my lifetime, I had purposefully avoided pain and suffering as often as possible. In relationships, I always left first—a reaction to my long denied feelings of abandonment. Consciously recognizing the child Persephone's pain of abandonment as my own, it reminded me of a book—*The Hero Within: Six Archetypes We Live By.* I found the book on my shelf and looked for the description of the Orphan archetype.

The author Carol Pearson described archetypes as deep and abiding patterns in the human psyche that remain powerful and present over time. She argued that we have six archetypes to live by—the Innocent, the Orphan, the Wanderer, the Warrior, the Martyr, and the Magician or Shaman—they each have a different point of view. These patterns are universal and appear in dreams, art, literature and myth. The ancients knew them as gods and goddesses. We know these archetypes because they live within us and if we deny them, they can possess us. These six particular archetypes, the author suggests, relate to our personal Hero's Journey. Each archetype has a task to complete before we move on. The journey begins with the trust of the Innocent, moves on to the longing for safety of the Orphan, to the self sacrifice of the Martyr, then to the exploring of the Wanderer, and the competition and triumph of the Warrior, and finally to the authenticity and wholeness of the Magician. The circular journey may take us around that cycle several times in our lifetime.

The first time I read this book, a few years earlier, I immediately jumped to the Warrior and Magician and swept the other archetypes under the rug of unconsciousness. Now, acknowledging the pain of abandonment made me look closer at the archetype of the Orphan.

Pearson states we move from the Innocent to the Orphan at the time of the Fall—the loss of trust—usually early in life. The dominant emotion of the Orphan's worldview is fear and the basic motivation is survival. Since I had survived an abortion attempt by my deserted pregnant teen-age mother who felt ashamed, afraid and alone, my *Fall* came very early—in the darkness of the womb. Unable to attach emotionally to my mother, I grew up feeling like the abandoned Orphan. This stage is so painful most people choose to escape by using various types of drugs, work, mindless pleasure or relationships or religion as means to dull the pain and provide a sense of safety. I had tried them all.

When I read that the Orphan yearns for a return to a primal innocence that is fully childlike, where a loving mother or father figure cares for every need, I recognized her. I still felt like that orphan yearning for her lost innocence.

Chapter Six

The Gift Of The Goddess

As I studied and wrote, my day started by walking down Rancho Mission Road to the gym near the Jack Murphy Stadium. I stood outside in line waiting for the doors to open at 6:00 AM. After riding the stationary bicycle a few miles to nowhere, I danced to Michael Jackson's *Thriller*. Walking home briskly up the road completed my workout. I showered, ate my breakfast, recorded my dreams, and then settled in about mid-morning to read my books, write my notes and continue my search for the Mother. Demeter's myth intrigued me, but it was not *my* myth. The pain of the abandoned child resounded deeply, but many more faces of the Goddess awaited my discovery. The trail moved from Greek to Egyptian mythology.

In the beginning Isis—the Goddess from whom all becoming arose, wrote the ancient Egyptians. All things feminine, the Goddess Isis was daughter, sister, wife and mother. Isis—daughter of Nuit, the Overarching Night Sky. Isis—sister of Nephthys, Goddess of the Underworld. Isis—sister and wife to Osiris, God of the Nile Waters and Vegetation. Isis—mother of the Sun, Horus. In about 2500 BCE, her attributes numerous and her powers limitless, Queen Isis ruled over Egypt with King Osiris.

The story goes that in those times Set—the God of Desert and Darkness, grew jealous of his mighty brother and tricked him into laying down in a coffin, nailed it shut, and then threw it into the Nile—sending Osiris to a watery grave. Her inconsolable scream penetrated the desert air when Isis learned of the deed. She keened in anguish. With Nephthys, her sister, Isis set sail to find the body of her king. The sisters sang woeful songs that echoed along the banks of the Nile and some say those lamentations can still be heard today.

After an arduous journey, the sisters found the body of King Osiris and sent it home. But Set managed to steal the body and cut it into fourteen pieces then scattered them abroad. Again, Isis searched and managed to find all the pieces of Osiris except the phallus, so she fashioned one of gold. Weeping over the body of her King, Isis sang love songs to her husband as she massaged his skin with sweet smelling oils. She restored his life and in the ecstasy of the moment became impregnated with their child Horus. Isis made the promise of immortality to Osiris and with him to all humanity: "You will live again, forever."

I recognized the theme. The Egyptian story predated Demeter and Persephone by over 1000 years, but the tale of betrayal, death, loss, search, lamentation, resurrection and a promise of immortality sounded similar, with a different set of characters. Looking through the images of Isis, I noticed her oft portrayed with outstretched wings reminiscent of a mother bird who would protect her flock. Over 2,500 years later, it is recorded that Jesus wept over Jerusalem and cried: "Oh Jerusalem, Jerusalem …how often would I have gathered thy children together even as a hen gathered her chickens *under her wings*, and ye would not!" (Matthew 23:37) And, Jesus was also betrayed, killed, mourned, anointed with oils, resurrected from the dead, and promised immortality—a recurring theme passing down through the ages.

About this time my flamboyant Auntie Mame in Los Angeles needed cataract surgery. She did not have children, and being her favorite niece—her *Pussywillow*—I drove from San Diego to help. The day of the surgery, we arrived at the hospital in Cerritos at 6:00 AM for pre-op procedures. The nurse told me to retrieve my aunt at 4:00 PM the same afternoon. I stayed 'til they gave her meds, then braved the morning traffic on the Long Beach Freeway to visit Carolyn—an old friend who lived in Altadena. Years ago, I had met her through personal friends when we both worked in Vocational Rehabilitation. Carolyn, a post polio survivor had lived with paraplegia since high school. This slim attractive woman finished college earning a Ph.D. in psychology and had been the highest woman political appointee during Governor Reagan's tenure—all in a wheelchair. She lived an independent life with the help of her husband Dick. We enjoyed a mutual admiration society—she impressed me as the brightest woman I knew and she loved my spiritual audacity. Now retired, I often visited with her and we shared an emotional bond.

I arrived early. We talked over tea and caught up on our latest pursuits. She loved hearing my dreams and adventures and stimulated me with the latest Rehab gossip and her innovative intellect. As we sat chatting in the dining room, a voice called out from the front door: "Carolyn, are you home?"

"Oh my goodness it's Mitch. What a surprise." She called back "Come on in, we're in the dining room."

I recognized the tall, handsome Greek with salt and pepper curly hair and a full gray mustache as he walked in the door, carrying cookies. He bent down and kissed Carolyn's light blond hair.

"It's good to see you, but why are you playing hooky?" She asked.

"I had a dentist appointment and was driving to work on the freeway when I saw the Arroyo Seco exit and thought of you. So here I am bearing gifts—Greek Koulouria cookies I baked. I saw the VW Rabbit outside and wondered if you had company."

"You remember Jacque don't you? She was a counselor in the Van Nuys office. Get a cup of coffee and sit down."

"Of course I remember Jacque. Who could forget her?" He looked at me and smiled. "You were the talk of Rehab when you took off for India. I have to say we all thought you were crazy." Mitch removed his jacket, poured some coffee and offered us some of his Greek cookies. "But I've kept track of you through Carolyn," he admitted almost shyly as he sat down.

While I worked in Rehab, I admired Mitch from afar—known as the fastest rising star in the Agency and the youngest Regional Administrator in the State. I'd see him at meetings and conferences and occasionally he and his wife and my husband and I attended the same social affairs.

"Oh yes, I remember you well, you were one of the big shots—a Greek hero," I said. "I left for India in '74, let's see that's been eleven years, how time flies." I smiled and felt a warm glow. "Catch me up on what's been happening in your world."

Mitch reported his life had taken a down turn since his popular days as the rising star. A change in State politics had shaken the Agency and left him on the wrong side of the tracks—he had been downsized. His voice lost its timbre as he spoke of a serious heart infection and that he and his wife had parted ways. It sounded like the Greek hero had been wounded, but in my mind his star still shown brightly. I remembered his intelligence, quick wit and authority—this strong man had always attracted me and now it seemed fate intervened. I munched on the anise-flavored cookies, licking the sesame seeds off my fingers as we talked. We laughed together and when he reached across the table, so did I—our hands touched.

The Goddess had sent me a Greek hero. Mitch was named after Miltiadis, the Greek general credited with the victory against the Persians in the Battle at Marathon in 480 BC. Later in another battle, Miltiadis was wounded and died in prison, but that is the fate of some heroes. Others die in battle and come home on their shield and still others grow old and fame fades. But in that moment, that wounded Greek hero grabbed my heart. After he settled his personal affairs we got married, witnessed by our mutual good friend Carolyn.

I never thought to marry again, never thought that any man would care for a feminist in pursuit of a feminine God, but then I underestimated the Great Goddess. She sent me a strong Greek Taurus Bull who baked cookies, loved to shop and cook, interpreted the Tarot Cards and read my fortune in the grounds of a Greek coffee cup. Mitch introduced me to Greece where he spoke the language well. He took me to the ground where I'd only been in my mind and I walked where the goddesses walked. We traveled three months—sailed to many Greek Islands and swam nude in the Aegean Sea. Visiting Delphi, I paid my respects to the First Mother Gaia, we roamed Athens and climbed the Parthenon where I cried at the demise of Athena. Touring the Peloponnese, we sat on a bench where the ancient Olympians waited to play, visited his father's hometown near Volos and found lost cousins. We drank lots of Ouzo and ate many mezze, but best of all Mitch danced like Zorba. When his Greek heritage filled his body and flowed to his feet, he came alive. At the end of the trip, he stayed in Cyprus, his mother's birthplace, while I flew to Egypt to meet Isis. When we returned home, we settled down in Carlsbad near San Diego and I continued my writing with new spunk and spirit. But I wasn't quite ready for what happened next.

Chapter Seven

The Dark Side Of The Goddess

One spring day in 1987, I came across a notice in the library for a Jungian bookfair and lecture by a local San Diego professor Christine Downing, author of *The Goddess—Mythological Images of the Feminine.* Excited about meeting like-minded people I attended the gathering at Claremont College expecting to delve deeper into images of the Great Mother Goddess.

Instead, I met Sekhmet—the ferocious Egyptian Lion-headed Goddess—her chilling image shocked me. In the lecture, Dr. Downing related that Ra, the Sun God of Upper Egypt, called on Sekhmet to destroy the mortals who conspired against him. The fierce feline Sekhmet spared no one in battle and acquired a taste for blood that could not be quelled. When she had killed all the enemies of Ra, she began destroying the rest of humanity and no one could stop her. In desperation, Ra tricked her by turning the Nile red like blood. However the red liquid was not blood, but beer mixed with pomegranate juice. Sekhmet, deceived by the color, drank up the liquid and became so intoxicated that she gave up the slaughter. Sekhmet fell into a deep sleep and when she awoke the rage had disappeared.

A Lion-headed Goddess with a thirst for blood on a killing spree—my imagination balked. Worse than the random unintentional killing by earthquake or boulder from Mother Nature, this story portrayed purposeful slaughter personified by a goddess. I didn't want to hear it. I didn't want to think about it. I had carefully avoided India's goddess Kali with skulls around her neck and daggers dripping blood from her hands, now I was confronted with a bloodthirsty Egyptian goddess. I sought to put that horrific image out of my mind. It took along time before I could face her.

Years later, in 1995, I found myself on a tour in Luxor, Egypt walking in an ancient tomb, listening to a dark haired, rather small Egyptologist. He explained the fragile and fading, but still visible, pictures painted on the tomb walls from stories in the Egyptian Book of the Dead. The guide spoke with authority, and I took copious notes. My fellow tourists looked bored. "This is Isis on the Nile." He pointed up to pictures of the woman in a boat.

I recognized the now familiar figure standing in an open skiff floating on a river. Then in the next scene, my eyes seemed to play tricks—in the place of Isis stood Sekhmet with a spear in her hand reaching out to kill a crocodile. "This is Isis killing Set, the God of the Underworld, represented by a crocodile. Set had murdered his brother Osiris by placing him in a coffin…," the guide went on with the story, but I had stopped listening. I stared at the wall. *This was not the loving, life-giving Isis!*

When the guide finished speaking I said, "But that's not Isis, you've made a mistake." The Egyptologist's soft brown eyes caught mine as he gently explained. "They are one—the Goddess of Life and Death." He continued, "Isis took on the form of Sekhmet whenever she needed that power and strength or wanted revenge."

The group moved on to the next panel; I stood alone facing Sekhmet. The child in me cringed, but the adult knew that one day I, too, needed to embrace this power, however difficult it seemed at the moment.

Chapter Eight

The Black Virgin

On that fall day in 1987 in Claremont when I first heard the story of Sekhmet, I also met the Black Virgin.

Glancing through the offerings piled high on the tables at the Book-fair, I searched for something to read with my sack lunch. "May I help you find a book?" smiled a slight, gray-haired man. He fit my impression of most *Friends of Jung*—scholarly and interesting.

"Just looking," I said, returning his smile. "I'm not sure exactly, but I've browsed through enough bookstores to know that what I need usually finds me." He nodded knowingly and moved away to help someone else.

Then, among the many stacks of hardbacks and soft covers, off in a corner, a paperback drew my eye. I stared at a crowned black queenly figure holding a crowned black child in her right arm and in her left hand, an upright sword. I picked it up and read—*The Cult of the Black Virgin*.

Flipping through the small book, the ebony queen on the cover would not let me go. "No choice," I laughed, "it has happened again." The kindly man returned and wrote up the sale. Then I found a place to sit on the grass in the sun, arranged my long skirt around my legs, unfolded my brown paper bag and reached in for my turkey croissant. Perusing the back cover I read this description.

"Why are over 400 of the world's images of the Madonna 'black' or 'dark'? And why are they so little known? *The Cult of the Black Virgin* investigates the pagan origins of the phenomenon as well as the heretical Gnostic-Christian underground stream which flowed west with the cult of Mary Magdalene and resurfaced in Catharism at the time of the Crusades."

Unwrapping my sandwich, my stomach made noise and my mind mused—*over four hundred images? Amazing! Where do Black Virgins come from? She doesn't look African. Why are they black? The words "black" and "virgin" seem contradictory. Could she possibly be a form of the Virgin Mary—the mother of Jesus, but then it says "pagan origins."* Feeling lightheaded, I bit into the soft croissant and crunched a stalk of celery. *What kind of Madonna carries a sword?*

Scanning further, a particular sentence in the Introduction caught my eye—"Joan of Arc now raised to the altars, and safely dead for five and a half centuries, was not in her lifetime a favorite daughter of the Church, though her *special devotion to the Black Virgins* would not have been viewed askance in her day."

That fateful day introduced me to three intertwined feminine figures who changed the course of my life—The Black Virgin, Sekhmet, and Joan of Arc.

Over the next few weeks, I poured over Ean Begg's *The Cult of the Black Virgin*. The book fascinated me. She was earth, rock, primal, native, nature—her blackness symbolic of the void, of night, of everywhere and nowhere—a mystery. The height of her popularity peaked in the 12th and 13th centuries when the Notre Dame Cathedrals dedicated to Our Lady were built in France, but reports of the Black Virgin's appearance dated back to AD 46.

About her origin—numerous theories prevailed citing many ancient goddesses, even Mary Magdalene. The simplest and most widely held theory on the Black Virgins in Europe surmised at the time of the Crusades, pagan statues of Isis nursing her infant Horus at her breast or with the child sitting on her lap were brought back from the East by returning warriors. These images evolved into the Madonna and Child. But to me, She was more than an image, She was, and *is,* an inspiring but disquieting presence.

Begg concluded the Black Virgin continued to be what she had been for some 30 millennia—the manifestation of the Great Goddess. Exploring her many possible personas and attributes, his book included Sekhmet, arguing that the personification of the chaotic darkness brings light out of ignorance. "Sekhmet's annihilating power makes conception possible—one form must die before another can come into being." I stopped reading and put down my book. *Could this be true?* The insight assuaged my fear of the destructive goddess Sekhmet and illumined further the enigmatic Dark Madonna. Begg's comparison to some of the Great Goddesses of Heaven and Earth helped me envision her compassion for death and her passion for life.

This Black Virgin who involved herself in the many aspects of life fascinated me. She combined the nurturing, healing, life-giving aspect of the feminine and the protective, warrior, aggressive aspects of the masculine. Her multifaceted persona encouraged me to embrace all those conflicting parts within myself that I had labeled as opposites. As a child, I felt that the devil and god were having a tug-of-war inside me. On the job, I felt honored when my boss said, "You think like a man"—the masculine mind being preferred over the feminine emotion. As a Baptist I didn't dance or drink, believing it was better to honor the spirit and ignore the body. As a young adult I marched for peace and abhorred war. As a nurse I sought to heal life and to avoid death—always the opposites. But this Black Virgin seemed to embrace the paradox of creation and destruction, of life and death—she represented a real force for change.

Politically, she has always been in favor of freedom and integrity, the rights of people, cities and nations as exemplified by the Black Madonna of Czestochowa known as the Queen of Poland. That Black Virgin still carries a scar on her right cheek slashed with a saber by a robber when he took the painting in 1430, then abandoned it when his horses refused to carry the stolen icon. This wounded Madonna inspired the great revolutionary leader Lech Walenska to fight the authoritative rigid rule and influenced Polish independence.

Another famous Dark Virgin—*Our Lady of Guadalupe* appeared in 1531 to a poor Indian peasant on the hill of Tepeyac, near the present Mexico City. The apparition asked for a shrine to be built on that spot in her honor. Guadalupe inherited the devotion formerly accorded to Tonantzin, the Aztec mother of the gods. She saved the Aztec people because they were required to bow to the conquistador's God or be killed. Centuries later, fighters for the Mexican Revolution against Spain seeking independence chanted, "Long Live Our Lady of Guadalupe" as they marched for their freedom with her banner held high.

In AD 430, at Le Puy France, a widow with a malignant fever saw a vision of the Virgin who told her to lay on top of a black flat stone from a dolmen —a prehistoric tomb consisting of a large flat stone laid across several upright rocks. Following these directions, the widow was healed of the fever. The Virgin then instructed that a church be built on that site in her honor. *Interesting*, I thought. *How often, new religions are built on ancient pagan ruins.* The black "fever-stone" sat on the church's high altar until replaced later by a wooden Black Virgin statue.

At that same Cathedral of Notre Dame in Le Puy, Pope Urban prepared for the First Crusade in 1095. An inspiration, a symbol and a rallying cry the soldiers carried the Black Virgin's banner singing "Salve Regina" when they set off to regain the Holy Land in Jerusalem. Begg states, "Nowhere does the Holy Virgin receive a more special and filial cult of respect, love and veneration."

The Cathedral of Notre Dame at Le Puy is the same place that in 1429, Joan of Arc sent her Mother and brothers to pray for her victory in Orleans during a Great Jubilee—again, Joan of Arc and the Black Virgin. Their connection intrigued me. Both of these revolutionary feminine figures resisted authority, were controversial, found their own path, and when necessary picked up the sword to fight a battle or otherwise sought discernment. Although the Black Virgin continued to be somewhat of an illusive mystery, the well documented history of Joan of Arc and her devotion to the Black Virgin gave me a different angle to pursue. Together they could teach me discernment—to know the time to use the pen and the time to pick up the sword.

Chapter Nine

Joan Of Arc

Over the next few months in 1988, I scoured public, private, and university libraries in pursuit of the interests stirred by that "little black paperback." I looked for common threads that connected it to my other interests. As part of my counseling practice, I had presented workshops on primordial and pre-Christian goddesses to the growing number of women interested in exploring the feminine face of god. Now I added two more exciting subjects to my research agenda—the Black Virgin and Joan of Arc. I had no idea how these jigsaw pieces would someday fit together and solve an amazing puzzle.

At the University of San Diego library, I sat for hours on uncomfortable wooden chairs and immersed myself in the mountain of books written about the stranger-than-fiction life of the Maid of Lorraine described by Mark Twain as "the most extraordinary person the human race has ever produced." Taking notes after looking through library files (before online research engines), I roamed the stacks and gathered volumes to take home for further attention.

While pursuing Joan's well-published life (it is said only the Bible has produced more written material than has Joan of Arc), I also followed clues about Joan's little known devotion to the Black Virgin. Joan sought the Virgin's shrines wherever possible along her military route and sent her mother and brothers to the Black Virgin at Le Puy to pray for her victory at Orleans.

The controversial *Holy Blood, Holy Grail* recommended by the author of *The Cult of the Black Virgin* provided further intriguing information. Apparently in the 11th to the 13th century, when the cult of the Black Virgin hit a peak of devotion, it connected with a similar cult to Mary Magdalene—some believed they were the same.

At times I felt overwhelmed trying to separate fact from fiction especially after discovering the alleged marriage of Jesus and Mary Magdalene and, if it is to be believed, some scholars suggest they left a royal bloodline—the Merovingians—that still exists in France today.

As my studies continued, I learned that the Priory of Sion, a secret organization founded in the 11th century, was dedicated to protecting and restoring this very same Merovingian royal bloodline to the throne of France. In addition, I uncovered links between the Priory of Sion, the Merovingians, Joan of Arc, and the Black Virgin. *Pretty heady stuff,* I thought to myself and wondered at the time where this pilgrimage would lead? Beyond the intrigue, something personal hung in the balance. An unrecognized vacuum in my soul longed to be filled. Over the next several years, combining discovered data with my own active imagination, I wrote a manuscript—*The Joan of Arc Legacy.*

After completing the book, I felt an urgency to travel to France, especially to Domremy—the place of Joan's birth. Somehow it seemed ludicrous for me to write about this 15th century savior from second-hand sources. I wanted to honor her birthplace, stand where she stood, walk in the fields where she heard her voices—to feel her presence as strongly as possible. This mystic, warrior and martyr drew me to her from around the world and through the centuries—and I came.

On October 31, 1992—All Hallowed Eve, I knelt before the baptismal font of Joan of Arc. At this sacred spot, I sought a blessing from the spirit of this heroine who inspired me. The recent addition of stained glass windows depicting the life and death of Joan added a poignant touch to the uniquely preserved church in her rural birthplace.

Looking up, I saw an image portraying Joan's last moments on earth as she burned at the stake. *Her peasant family could never have imagined at her baptism that in less than 20 years this innocent would die a horrible death at the hands of the English with the approval of the Church.* I closed my eyes, repelled by the grim scene. I envisioned the cruelty of Joan's sacrifice and winced at the cost she chose to pay. My tears could not wash away her hurt or mine.

"Joan," I pleaded. "What can I write about you that has not already been written?" I listened to the silence, and then an answer came from everywhere and nowhere. "*Do not write about what I did, but who I am.*"

I had already written the details of *what* this 15th Century heroine had accomplished, now she urged me to delve deeper into the *who* behind the *what*.

The Cult of the Black Virgin—which inspired my interest in Joan of Arc as well as the Black Virgin—had been published in 1985 and in his book Begg referred extensively to *Holy Blood, Holy Grail* written in 1982. Later, in 2004 when Dan Brown published his phenomenal best-seller *The Da Vinci Code,* he relied heavily on the same material and came to similar conclusions—our paths must have crossed in the night.

In *The Joan of Arc Legacy* I took a further step with the hypothesis that Joan, with the help of the Priory of Sion, led the way to return the royal bloodline to the throne of France. Joan helped crown the dauphin as King Charles II and his son Louis carried the Merovingian blood from his mother's lineage. King Louis XI, who reigned after his father's death, was known to have a great affection for the Black Virgin and regarded Mary Magdalene as the mother of the royal line of France.

Brown stirred many conservative Christians and the Catholic Church with his novel. In the following conversation about the Holy Grail, Sophie looked at Da Vinci's *The Last Supper*:

> Sophie scanned the work eagerly. "Does this fresco tell us *what* the Grail really is?"

> "Not *what* it is," Teabing whispered. "But rather *who* it is. The Holy Grail is not a thing. It is, in fact . . . a *person."*

The dialogue reminded me of Joan's distinction between *what* she did and *who* she is. *The Da Vinci Code* discussion goes on to state that the Holy Grail represented the sacred feminine and the lost goddess. Then Teabing shocks Sophie when he tells her that the Holy Grail is Mary Magdalene. He continues by describing the legacy of a smear campaign launched by the early Church to defame her in order to cover up the dangerous secret—Mary Magdalene's role as the bride of Jesus and mother of their royal bloodline. Mary Magdalene—labeled a prostitute, revealed as Lover and Mother—embracing the paradox.

Sophie had no idea at that moment that this revelation referred to her personally, that she carried the sacred bloodline and was a daughter of Mary Magdalene. Likewise, I had no idea at the moment of my discovery that I, as a woman, was also linked to the Holy Grail as a daughter of the Sacred Feminine.

What happened to the Black Virgin, to the sacred feminine legacy? Did the Church's sweeping *witch-hunts* and the barbaric Inquisition drive the sacred feminine into the underground or did history intervene—the French Revolution? I believe that Joan's mission continued a mystical lineage that began with the primordial Great Goddess, who through the centuries has manifested at times and at other times has remained hidden in the underground stream. She has never disappeared, but speaks to all that have the ears to hear.

Looking at the picture whose pieces had now come together, I felt the epiphany of the moment called for communion with the Holy Grail and toasted her with a glass of red wine.

Chapter Ten

Safely Home, Friends

A few months before the Joan of Arc pilgrimage and the psychopomp workshop, friends and family arrived from near and far to help me celebrate my 60th birthday. I rented a house next door for the guests from Northern California, Denver, Honolulu and my sister from Indiana. During the weekend they recognized and honored me as a *Crone*—a woman of age, wisdom and power. On Saturday we performed rituals and on Sunday a Dixieland Jazz band blared and I even sang while a Mexican Restaurant catered a brunch. I felt royally *croned*. (Looking back, I wonder if embracing my age, wisdom and power helped set the stage for my experience in the psychopomp workshop— issues of death and dying may be the crone's prerogative.)

On Sunday evening, the overnight guests gathered in my living room continuing the festivities when Kurt, my neighbor, dropped by with a bottle of wine wrapped in a purple colored gift bag labeled *To The Ancient One*. The slight, fair thirty-four year old young man smiled when he handed it to me. "I wish I could have joined the party today, but I haven't been feeling well lately. I had to quit my job," he swallowed and looked down and mumbled softly, "I have AIDS."

"Oh Kurt!" I put my arms around his shoulders and hugged him. "I'm so sorry. I did notice that you've lost weight, but I had no idea. I *am* so sorry," I repeated, not knowing what else to say.

"That's okay," Kurt responded. "I didn't want to mention it. You know how some people are, even my priest has turned his back, but I thought you'd understand." He stood there looking so vulnerable. I wondered how the conservative neighbors would respond to the news.

"If there's anything I can do," I stammered the old cliché, but really meant it. "I'll come over and have tea soon," I said smiling, "if I'm not too feeble. This Ancient One thanks you for the birthday present. You know how I love a good Cabernet and this is a great one."

That night began a journey that the two of us traveled together over the next several months. One day I mentioned the psychopomp workshop I had taken, hesitantly speaking of my experience with Barbara's troubled soul. "I really believe that preparing for your death can help alleviate the fear," I explained.

The story fascinated Kurt and he asked hesitantly: "Would you help me when my time comes?"

"Of course, I would be honored," I agreed, relieved at his positive response.

Then the disciplined German Kurt asked: "Could we practice?"

Visiting regularly, I sat by his bed and read to him. We discussed near death experiences—accounts of people who had clinically died and returned to tell the tale. Together we talked of looking for the light and of loved ones waiting. Sometimes Kurt didn't want to talk, but put on his favorite CD opera and lay back to listen. I just sat quietly as the music surrounded us both in a protective cocoon.

As the days passed, Kurt's immune system slowly collapsed and the disease progressed; he moved inevitably closer to the threshold. Sometimes I just sat by his bedside while he slept; I had become a friend to his soul, a witness to his dying. It took away some of the terror. Kurt no long feared his death.

"I want to say my good-byes now," he told me, "so I can let go when my time comes. I hope my soul doesn't hang around. You'll help me, won't you?"

"Of course I'll be there for you," I assured him.

After a few weeks, he needed more care than his partner, Juan, could provide; Kurt moved to Hospice House. Shortly thereafter I got a call that Kurt was failing and could I come. I hurried over. A burley man wearing a black support belt with his arms full of linens opened the door. I asked to see Kurt. He nodded and pointed the way. Entering the darkened room, I saw a grief-stricken Juan, lying in bed beside his dying lover—holding him gently in his arms. Kurt's stoic German parents sat close by. I knelt at Kurt's bedside and took his frail hand in mine. He opened his eyes and smiled. "Look for the light. Don't be afraid." I reminded him of what we had practiced.

Kurt slipped away peacefully within a few minutes. Juan looked at me, his voice breaking. "He waited for you," he said, smiling through his tears. Together we gazed at Kurt's tranquil face. I stood up and hugged Juan and then expressed my sympathy to the parents before walking out of the room in a daze.

The stocky male nurse approached and asked, "Are you Jacqueline?" I nodded my head. "He wasn't afraid you know. He told me you helped him. Thank you."

Kurt was the first of several people I helped to cross over as I volunteered with the San Diego AIDS project, but my real calling seemed to come from those who had already died, especially if the death had been tragic or unexpected.

A few months later in 1993, I traveled a day early to a conference in Washington D.C. in order to visit the recently opened Holocaust Memorial Museum. I arrived at the Memorial on a cold November morning and stood freezing in a long line with other anxious tourists.

Upon entering the museum, each visitor received a card inscribed—*For the dead and the living we must bear witness.* Mine held the picture and life story of a 40-year-old wife and mother named Ilse who perished in Auschwitz. The museum provided names and faces to the holocaust victims.

When I approached an old railroad boxcar that once carried countless victims to the death camps, I hesitated. The doors stood open. Although it looked empty, I envisioned the memories it held—whimpering babies carried by starving mothers, frail elderly, gaunt men and women crammed together and prodded like cattle by sadistic soldiers. Most of the tourists gazed reluctantly or shied away, some ventured to touch the surface of the boxcar with tears in their eyes. I felt compelled to enter. Alone, with the lingering scent of fear surrounding me, I heard cries echoing from anguished voices begging for help. The faceless misery of humanity saturated the very timber of the boxcar and left me weak.

This encounter reinforced my psychopomp experience. I did not doubt that many suffering souls continue to wander seeking justice. I asked myself, *How many people are willing to help them? It's certainly not for everyone.* I offered a prayer and walked away with a heavy heart. I didn't know it, but my work lay elsewhere.

The next day I took a taxi to the Vietnam Veterans Memorial Wall where I expected more lost souls would be waiting. I stood in awe staring at the Wall that held the inscribed names of 58,400 United States lost veterans that served in the Vietnam War from 1959 to 1975. I sensed the presence of ghosts hovering in the area—possibly soldiers wanting to remain near their buddies. I remembered how the antagonism over Vietnam divided people and dishonored many veterans. The following day, I ordered the *Vietnam Veterans Memorial Directory of Names* to be sent to my home. When it arrived, I divided the 58,400 names by 365. Every day for the next year I called the names of 160 men or women—their rank and service, their date and place of birth, and date of *casualty*, as the book called it. Starting with Gerald L. Aadland from Sisseton SD born March 29, 1945—died May 30, 1968 to David Lee Zywicke from Manitowoc WI born December 4, 1947—died December 7, 1967, I thanked each veteran for his or her sacrifice, surrounded the soul with light, and offered a blessing. I also asked if they wanted to move on (it's important to ask). Then I prayed that each soul be at peace. The staggering millions of holocaust victims had overwhelmed me, but this I could do. I whispered, "Safely home, friends."

Chapter Eleven

Spanish Ancestors

My practice of guiding departed souls continued. In addition to the Vietnam Veterans, I looked for the victims of tragedy or unexpected death in the newspaper. Reading about a plane crash or a murder, I would sit in meditation and quietly call the name of each person, seek a blessing for the soul and pray for its safe return home.

In 1993, Mitch and I moved from the ocean coast in Carlsbad, California to the mountains in Bend, Oregon to be near my children. The lack of nurturing and stability in my own family, both as a child and as a parent, left me with a desire to live in close proximity to my daughter and son and be a loving presence in the lives of my four grandchildren.

In the fall of 1994, I sought more information and experience about my psychopomp work and decided to attend another Shamanic Death and Dying workshop.

Michael Harner, the founder and director of the Foundation for Shamanic Studies, led the class. During the workshop, Michael reminded us that the shamanic tradition considers birth and death to be connected like a circle. When the soul comes into this life and runs its life course, it must return home to its source, but some souls have difficulty and need help along the way. We took several shamanic journeys accompanied by the beat of the drum to explore different realms of nonordinary reality.

We prepared for our experience to guide a restless soul still attached to the physical plane. My power animals—a hawk and a lion and my spirit guide—*She Who Honors,* riding a white horse—accompanied me on my shamanic journeys.

On the first journey to the middleworld, Michael asked us to just visit and explore the territory. He suggested that we might look for a deceased loved one. I hoped to find my father Joe or *Justinano* as his family named him. When I saw his ghostly apparition, I barely recognized him. He was with his three brothers—Solly, George and Clarence, his father—Ubaldo Isadore known as U.I., and the grandfather—Jesus.

They all seemed to be waiting for me, stuck in the middleworld because of their ancestral family karma—the long suppression of the Native Americans in New Mexico. Before I could speak, the drumbeat called me back from the journey. I remembered my Aunt Mame telling me that my great-grandfather Jesus had kept the indigenous people as servants, but treated them like slaves. He carried a whip and used it often as he rode on horseback around his ranch. He forbid her from playing with *the heathens* and considered them less than human.

Michael then talked more about the middleworld and the possible scenarios of why souls remained there. He stated that unhappy souls could enter other people's bodies and that hauntings and poltergeists are often confused souls in the middleworld. He instructed us on how to help guide a soul, but cautioned it might take more than one attempt.

The drumbeat began again. We started our next journey with the intent of guiding a soul out the middleworld. I returned to my father and his family. Now they seemed to be on an island with a mountain in the background. My father's spirit came to me and said I had a role to play in helping to dispel the family's negative energy by honoring the Native American tradition.

"I never really knew you," he looked at me almost as a stranger. "I couldn't love you because no one ever loved me. My mother died when I was only three. Please forgive me for my rude behavior and physical abuse. I knew no other way." His apparition lamented, "We've waited so long. We've been caught in the web of misusing the male power passed from one generation to the next. Only a female can break that spell. It is yours to do."

The release had to come through the shamanic tradition because it had been so dishonored. And, there I was in a shamanic workshop learning how to guide departed souls.

My father's voice continued, "You've been led to find your *true work* so you could release our family."

I assisted the apparition of my father onto my spirit guide's white horse and placed myself in front to help him. The hawk flew overhead leading the way. The lion and *She Who Honors* walked beside. We moved up the mountain, through a cave, and out into the light. Then it was time for him go on alone. At first my father seemed reluctant, then he asked me to tell his wife that the money she sent me helped make this possible. (His wife mailed $7,000.00 to me about the time I built a yurt for my shamanic practice.) He also gave me a message for my mother—*He was sorry for any pain that he caused her.*

His youngest brother Solly called out as we started up the hill wanting to join us. My father asked if I would go back and guide the rest of his family out of the middleworld. I promised that I would. He thanked me, turned and walked on in the light.

Upon my return home I spent time in the yurt taking each of the other family members, one by one, on the journey up the mountain, through the cave, and into the light.

Early in 1995, my mother called me from Florida to say my brother Everett in California had been diagnosed with late stage cancer. She wanted to visit him and asked me to join her. The next week I took the Amtrak train from Chemult, Oregon down the pacific coast to Los Angeles. Everett's son picked me up and drove me to their home.

"I'm dying!" My brother gasped when he saw me, his voice only a hoarse whisper due to the large tumor in his throat. His eyes filled with terror as he silently begged me to do something or contradict him.

"I know you're dying," I surprised myself by saying. "How do you want to die? Do you want to die consciously or do you want to be unconscious and free of pain?"

"No pain, *please!*" he rasped, and the look in his eyes changed from terror to a sorrowful plea.

I spent the next two days as my brother's spiritual midwife—the work I felt called to do. Spiritual midwifery includes soulwork *before* a person dies as well as after. It clears the way, loosens attachments, and assists in a process that allows the soul to move freely to a new space. In this case I helped my brother die in peace.

Everett did not speak another word after his first outcry to me. His wife called in hospice so he could receive comfort care and be free of pain. They brought a hospital bed and we placed it in the living room. He lay in silence. My 60-year-old brother had battled with heroin and alcohol abuse over the years and had given his wife and six children a difficult time, but they loved him and now he was dying. I held *sacred space* for his soul to do its work in its own way. *Holding sacred space* is a meditative state in which I sit in silence with someone and call on spiritual guidance for that person's *highest good*.

Two years my junior, Everett grew up rebellious acting a hellion. We fought like two cats in a gunnysack. I believe we made a pact before we came into this world—he would take the role of *very bad boy* allowing me the role of *very good girl* by comparison. And, when his time came, I would know what to do and be there for him to help clean up his mess. In those two days, I never left the house and witnessed a total transformation of his anger and fear into peace and liberation. He died consciously without pain surrounded by a family who loved him. I whispered, "Safely home, brother."

Chapter Twelve

More Than A Dream

My husband had a fear of dying and often wondered in amusement how he got hooked up with me. But Mitch was my tether—his love and his belief in my dreams allowed me to explore the unknown and return safely home. He respected my soulwork, but did not want to talk about it. I tried to do my spiritual practice before dawn or in the yurt, so that it did not intrude in his life. When I volunteered at the Humane Society to sit and comfort the dogs being given lethal injections due to overpopulation, Mitch rebelled and one day he asked me: "Do you know what it's like living with Digger O'Dell? You know who he is don't you?"

"Yes," I answered. "He was the 'Friendly Undertaker' in the Fibber McGee and Molly radio show back in the '40s.'" I laughed, but felt stung *He doesn't understand me,* I sulked.

That night Mitch took me out to Chan's Chinese Restaurant, trying to sooth my ruffled feathers. I continued to pout as we ate dinner in silence. When the fortune cookies came, I broke mine open and began to laugh uncontrollably and handed my paper fortune across the table. It read—*You shall be successful in all your undertakings.* Mitch smiled and said, "I give up," and never mentioned Digger O'Dell again.

After remembering the names of all the lost Vietnam Veterans, I solicited the names of AIDS victims from special interest groups, knowing many of them died without the support of their families or the comfort of their church. Friends who understood my work began to call with names of people they knew who had died in unusual circumstances and might need help. And, unfortunately I continued to find an ongoing supply of tragic deaths in the newspapers.

Although this practice might seem grim or depressing, it did not consume me. I had the ability to compartmentalize and mentally separate many tasks. Setting time aside in the quiet early morning and in the solitude of meditation, I held sacred space to honor these departed souls, released them to the light, and then went on my way.

"I had the craziest dream last night," I reported to my husband one morning at breakfast. "It was really weird. I was nursing a baby white seal at my breast. It had such soulful eyes."

Living with me through the years, nothing surprised Mitch, especially my dreams. "Do you know what they call those seals?" he asked.

"No." I didn't have a clue.

"Harp seals."

"Harp seals? That's interesting," My mind quickly flashed to the book *Women Who Run With the Wolves* in which Clarissa Pinkola Estes relates myths and stories of the Wild Woman Archetype. I went to my library and found the book. "Let me read this to you," I said to Mitch. "Within every woman there is a wild and natural creature, a powerful force, filled with good instincts, passionate creativity, and ageless knowing. Her name is Wild Woman. Wild life and the Wild Woman are both endangered species." I added, "Ain't that the truth."

"Sounds like your kind of book," Mitch smiled. "What does it have to do with the Harp Seals?"

"Here it is in *Sealskin, Soulskin*." I flipped through the table of contents. "Listen to this: 'The seal is one of the most beautiful of all symbols for the wild soul.' As I recall the story," I went on, "it's about a lonely hunter who wanted a human companion. He lived near the sea and one night he spied a small group of women dancing on a large rock near the shore. The women were seals who had dropped their skins to dance. The man stole one of the skins and then asked the woman to be his bride and live with him. He said in seven years he would return her skin and so she went with him. In time they had a child, but over the years without her sealskin, the woman began to dry out and become weak."

"Did the man give it back to her?" Mitch asked.

"No, he broke his promise and refused to return her sealskin afraid she would leave him and the child. But then the child accidentally found the skin and gave it to his mother. She pulled it on, scooped up the child and headed toward the sea. Breathing into his lungs, she carried the child deep into her watery home, but after seven days, he had to return to land. It wasn't his time to stay."

Mitch poured himself some coffee and asked, "So what does this have to do with your dream?"

"I know it sounds strange, but I think the baby seal in my dream is *my* wild soul and playing the harp will feed it. In the story the sealskin represents the soulskin. When the child found it and gave it to his mother, she could return home to the sea. Then she filled the child's lungs with her own breath so he could bridge two worlds—moving between land and sea. My dream seal could symbolize that part of myself that can walk between worlds—the psychopomp. It may also represent the harp whose vibrations can carry the soul home."

"I do associate harps with angels," Mitch offered.

"Do you remember when I told you about that woman who played the harp for people who were dying? The sound of the harp brought them comfort and seemed to help them die in peace. Maybe harp music could help *me* in my psychopomp work."

"Well, you have to get one first and learn how to play it," Mitch replied.

In one of those moments of serendipity, shortly after our talk, I read about a weekend class offered by our local college on the healing power of music—including the harp. I attended. When I touched the harp for the first time and gently ran my fingers across the strings, it released a crescendo of sounds that caressed my soul. Within a month I had purchased my own harp and began lessons.

The Harp Seal dream came in January 1997. Later that year I joined the two-year International Harp Therapy Program where students learn how to use the harp as a therapeutic tool to comfort and heal the body and soul. I began to play simple harp melodies as part of my spiritual practice. The sealskin—my soulskin— and the harp strings became intertwined nourishing each other.

The previous summer, a devastating fire had swept through our Sundance Ranch area. My daughter's home burnt to the ground and galloping flames consumed many of the juniper and pine trees on our five acres and left the surrounding forest scarred. My daughter's family lived in our guesthouse as they rebuilt.

In 1998, as things readjusted on the outside, a restless spirit stirred on the inside. Wanderlust called. I traveled to the mountains of Colorado and the deserts of New Mexico hoping to intuitively feel the draw of the place that had called. After narrowing it to the land of my ancestors in New Mexico, my husband came with me as we searched for our next home. Not too happy about moving Mitch grumbled, but he had made a commitment and by now knew living with me presented an adventure and he had signed on for the ride. He truly loved me.

We built a self-sustaining solar home on an old rancho with 40 acres, located in Mountainair, the center of a triangle between three Native American Pueblo ruins. We moved a few miles from Valencia where my father's family had lived and where my grandmother had died in 1912. Our malamute dog Wolf and three cats—The Queen, a regal Siamese—Guy, a large tabby—and B.C. a feral longhaired Siamese—accompanied us. We acquired a few goats and ducks to occupy the old barn (Mitch loved the goats), built a straw bale wall around the garden to keep out the coyotes and critters and settled down to see what would come next.

Exploring the land of my ancestors, I found a churchyard where I recognized the family names on some tombstones. "Are you looking for someone?" asked a caretaker. "There are more graves in the back. There was a flood here several years ago and some things got moved around."

"Thank you," I said and made my way through the weeds to the neglected side of the church. I gasped and almost stumbled over a damaged tombstone reading: "Rosella C Romero de Sanchez Born July 13, 1881—Died December 12, 1912"—my grandmother's grave.

On the morning of April 21, 1999, I awoke from an unsettling dream. *In the first scene, I am planning a memorial in a big church for my grandmother Rosella. In the dream I orchestrate the caterers, choir, and ushers and am responsible for the whole affair. I visit the crypt to view my grandmother's body. I see a curled mummy-like, brown and wrinkled figure begin to move. Her legs stretch out. A midwife comes and pulls a birthing baby from her womb, tears the umbilical cord in two and takes the baby away. My grandmother shrinks back into her mummy-like pose. Stones fall in place behind and around her forming a tombstone of sorts and she seems to be at peace. But I know this scene repeats itself every time someone views the body. The service is scheduled at 1:00 o'clock and the church quickly fills with guests, but her children have not arrived. I want to save a special place for them and reserve a bench in the back. The service begins. The choir sings a song about a Jubilee and people cry. Finally the children arrive, but the service is almost over. Irritated, I ask why they are late. They complain that the service was at a bad time. I reminded them that it had been planned for months and asked them to view the body. I wanted them all to see Rosella C Romero de Sanchez. The dream ended.*

I lay in bed reliving the excruciating scene of my grandmother giving birth over and over again. She was trapped between worlds unable to move onto the light. I realized this is why I had to come to New Mexico—to honor my grandmother and release her soul. I wondered if it was her voice that called me. She was waiting. I had come. It was mine to do. In the dream I had planned the memorial for months. The children arrived late seeming not to properly honor their mother. But I insisted that they see her, to recognize her and to know of her sacrifice. She had been forgotten. *My poor grandmother,* I sighed.

Later that day, honoring her life and her death, I played the harp to caress her soul with musical vibrations, and then released her into the light. Calling the parish priest at the Sangre de Cristo Catholic Church in Valencia where she lay buried, I arranged for a memorial mass to be conducted for her on Mother's Day. Mitch and I repaired her damaged tombstone in the churchyard and placed on it a statue of the Virgin Mother Mary who understood my grandmother's suffering.

When I discovered the Sangre de Cristo Catholic Church had celebrated a 50-year Jubilee in 1992, I remembered that in my dream the choir sang about a Jubilee. The past few years, like pieces of a puzzle, fell into place. A compelling picture of my spiritual journey emerged.

1992—The same year as the Jubilee, I celebrated my 60th birthday and honored myself as a crone—a woman of age, wisdom and power. Later that year I visited Joan of Arc's place of birth in France. Upon returning, I attended my first Shamanic Death and Dying Workshop and learned to walk between worlds and guide departed souls.

1993—I visited the Vietnam Veterans Memorial Wall and met more restless souls and the following year remembered each one.

1994—I found my father, grandfather, great-grandfather and three uncles trapped between worlds and guided them to the light.

1995—I acted as my brother's spiritual midwife and held sacred space for him as he peacefully died.

1996—The Sundance Ranch fire unsettled our lives.

1997—I dreamt of the baby white seal and the harp added another dimension to my spiritual midwifery practice.

1998—I felt the call to New Mexico.

1999—Seven years from the time I first accepted my Grandma Mary Jo's legacy to guide troubled souls, my Grandmother Rosella's spirit—stranded between worlds for over 86 years—came to me in a dream. I guided her to the light. "Safely home, grandmother."

Part Three

Coming Home

Chapter One

Bringing Repose

A few months before we moved to New Mexico, my mother's brother, Garmon, died of heart complications in Tennessee. Shortly after the troubling dream of my Grandmother Rosella, my Uncle Garmon showed up in a dream and appeared to be in a place that looked like a Las Vegas gambling casino. I knew that Garmon had been an addicted gambler during his life and had left a gambling debt when he died.

Since my first psychopomp experience in 1992, with the exception of my grandmother, the departed souls I guided had either appeared on a shamanic journey in a workshop or I had sought them out because they had died tragically or without warning. My Uncle Garmon did not fit in these categories—he died peacefully in the hospital.

As I meditated on the message of this dream and re-envisioned it, I sensed my uncle could not leave this gambling casino. *Aha!* I thought. *Maybe his psychological addiction to gambling is keeping his soul trapped between worlds so that he cannot move on to the light.*

In the dream, my uncle did not ask for help like my friend Barbara or my father's family when I met them on shamanic journeys nor did he appear in distress like my grandmother. I believed Garmon came into my dream seeking help. I surrounded him in light and prayed for his healing, but wondered if I could do more.

In my meditation I heard the words—*play a requiem for Garmon.* I looked up the word "requiem" in the dictionary, it stated: "a musical setting for the repose of the souls of the dead." Since playing the harp seemed beneficial in releasing the soul of my grandmother, I decided to play for my uncle and gathered a few inspiring songs. Either the mode or melody, the intent of the author, or an important memory guided my selection. I created a meaningful requiem—a Requiem for Garmon.

Minor chords—often interpreted as sad and dark or introspective—attracted me. I played a single note melody line with my right hand, accompanied by a simple chord or drone—one continuous sound—with my left hand. Creating a sacred space, I set my intent, plucked the harp strings, and let the healing vibrations surround Garmon's lost soul.

The first song—*Searching For Lambs,* reminded me of the Good Shepherd who left his flock to find the lost, lonely lamb and bring it home. Next, I played *The Foggy Dew* as sometimes mist gathers around the veil between worlds. Then out of the fog comes *Three Ravens,* symbolically known as messengers from beyond. As the clouds began to clear, I envisioned *The Great Silkie* appearing in the ocean's haze. The Silkies or sea folk are said to inhabit the Orkney Islands and Hebrides. These enchanted creatures dwell in the depths of the sea. The Silkie occasionally comes to land as a man to sire a child and then quickly disappears back into the briny deep. Later he returns to claim his child and takes it home to the sea.

This song reminds me of our own souls who bide their time on this earth in human form until the moment they are called to return home. The following song, *Seal Lullaby,* brings a few comforting moments as the notes beckon the soul to rest in the arms of the sea. Next, I played a 13th Century *Contiga,* dedicated to Our Lady, the Holy Virgin—the compassionate Divine Feminine who understands our pain and suffering. And, finally strumming *Farewell,* I whispered "Safely Home, Friend." After creating this Requiem for Garmon, I played it for all the departed souls in my spiritual practice and more departed friends and loved ones started showing up in my dreams.

One night I dreamt of Harry, the older gentleman who had once been my lover, he never forgave me for leaving him. Recently, I had learned of his passing, he had left money for me in his will. (I used it to build a studio retreat on our property in New Mexico where I could meditate and write.) In the dream he was pacing in an airport, wandering from window to window looking out at the incoming planes. Lying awake after rousing from the dream, I realized *he couldn't leave the airport*. His inability to find the incoming passenger left him frustrated. I suspected that he watched for me to come back. His unrealistic attachment, plus his anger and pride, ensnared him between worlds—waiting. I got up and played the requiem on my harp, sending prayers for his healing and release, then surrounded him with light and wished him Godspeed.

Another night a good friend from high school who had died of cancer the previous year made an appearance in a dream—she was surfing. Elaine lived in Hawaii and loved to surf and loved life. She had told me that sixty-nine was too young to die and did everything in her power to survive—took every drug, traveled to every doctor or program that promised a cure. In the dream she couldn't get off the surfboard, over and over, she rode the waves. I surmised that her passion for life and inability to accept her death had kept her spirit lingering between worlds unable to move on. My heart went out to my friend and I played my requiem for the repose of her soul.

Another night a high school chum, the local football hero, surfaced in my dream unable to leave the football field. I remembered his addiction to the applause of his adoring fans. After graduation nothing in his life ever quite measured up to that kind of adoration. He couldn't let go of the ball and needed someone to take his hand and guide him off the field. I gladly obliged.

Others appeared in my dreams—old friends, acquaintances, people I knew—and that seemed to be the criteria—I needed to *know* the nature of the attachment so I could help release them.

Then came the unspeakable tragedy of 9/11—September 11, 2001. I watched the television, mesmerized by the destructive scenes of collapsing buildings, smoke and dust rising from crushed concrete, fire fighters rushing into the holocaust while terrified survivors clamored to get out. I tore myself away from the television to light a candle in that *dark night of the soul* and then sat down to my harp. Tears flowed while the towers crumbled and souls stirred. My fingers moved to play

Searching for Lambs knowing that the Good Shepherd was there—in the chaos—searching.

Later that night I wrote in my journal: "I am so grateful that I could play the requiem because I believe that souls are born on their own note or vibration and at the moment of transition can be safely carried back home on that same note. I know that as the harp sounds the notes, the vibrations lift the soul like the wings of an eagle to soar between heaven and earth, giving new meaning to the phrase—music of the spheres.

How do I know that these departed souls need help? How do I know that the requiem brings repose to their souls? Can I prove it? No, of course I can't prove it. But in my world, I believe it is true. I believe we all have a purpose in this life and this is mine to do.

Chapter Two

Coming Home

Moving to central New Mexico in 1999 and settling in Mountainair, a small town sitting in a triangle of three Native American Pueblo ruins, did not seem like an accident. "Here in this remote, quiet valley, the silence belies the remarkable human history of this place," reads a guidebook from the Salinas Pueblo Missions National Monument. An ultimately tragic drama unfolded here in the seventeenth century, when the expanding empire of Spain finally reached these peaceful farming communities of Abo, Quarai and Gran Quivira.

The Pope made Spain responsible for converting natives to the Holy Catholic Church. Franciscan priests came looking for souls and the king's men demanded bodies for labor. The natives who were forced to build huge sanctuaries and other related tasks did not have time left to work for their own sustenance and eventually faced drought, famine and disease. Everyone lost. Hunger drove the Spaniards and the natives alike to abandon these once peaceful pueblos.

I believed my call to the land of my ancestors involved not only the release of my grandmother's soul, but also the amelioration of the suffering and pain brought to the land and indigenous people by those Spanish ancestors. The tall crumbling walls stood as monument to the false presumption that the god of brick and mortar could conquer a god honored in a *kiva,* the underground ceremonial chamber used by these Pueblo descendents of the Anasazi (ancient ones). These indigenous people made no clear distinction between the secular and the sacred. Planting corn and beans was as much a religious act as praying for the rain to help them grow. Life depended on both.

Many hours I spent wandering the dusty paths of those weathered mission remains, listening to the wind rustle through the roofless churches. I expected to encounter restless native spirits, but that was my own ignorance. As far as I could surmise the indigenous people had never lost touch with their own Great Spirit and had something to teach me. As I sat on those deserted broken walls my harp sounded haunting vibrations echoing in the silence. I played for my own lost indigenous soul.

Along with playing the harp, I also studied views of life after death from other traditions complementing my own shamanic spiritual practice. *The Tibetan Book of Living and Dying* by Sogyal Rinpoche offered understandable Buddhist practices to help people of any spiritual persuasion live more fully, die more peacefully, and make their way through the afterlife.

The Purification of the Six Realms—a practice that can be used in life or in a spiritual ritual with the dead, I found particularly helpful and modified it for my own use. It employs visualization and meditation to purify the body of the six main negative emotions that accumulate at particular energy centers in the body—also known as chakras. The emotion of anger is believed to be located at the soles of the feet, avarice or greed gathers at the base of the trunk, ignorance at the navel, doubt rests at the heart, jealousy at the throat, and pride rests at the crown of the head.

Rinpoche advises that traditional Buddhist practices such as this require special training, but I took the idea of it—the cleansing of harmful and possibly addicting emotions and their release—into my practice and accompanied the ritual with harmonic chords on the harp.

First, I cleansed my own negative emotions before offering myself as a channel for healing others. Then I envisioned the troubled soul, such as my Uncle Garmon, and brought light from above through his body down to the soles of his feet. Next I imaged all the karma (self-created destiny) created by his anger dissolve into the light. I moved to the base of the trunk and imaged all the karma created by his greed dissolve into the light. I continued with the same procedure at each realm—ignorance at the navel, doubt at the heart, jealously at the throat and pride at the crown of the head. At the end of the practice, I *saw* with my mind's eye, the entire being surrounded in radiant light.

In the previous year, studying with the International Harp Therapy Program, I had learned that sound and music are effective and simple means to clear and restore balance to an individual's energy system. In his book *Sacred Sounds,* Ted Andrews states that the chakras and their electromagnetic emanations respond to specific musical tones and vocalizations. "This can be done to facilitate healing, intuition, dream enlightenment, communing with spirits, or for invoking divine presence." I found certain chords effective with the different chakra points and added those harmonics at each of the six realms. This ritual added a new dimension to my shamanic psychopomp work as I performed a cleansing for each soul before playing the requiem.

I also revisited *The Egyptian Book of the Dead* remembering my pilgrimage to Egypt and the excursions to the tombs that held the ancient mysteries. I looked for similarities with the Native American Shamanic and the Buddhist teachings believing there must be a core of time-honored wisdom that could be synthesized to enrich our current understanding of the difficult subject of death. From these age-old traditions, I discovered a core of eight basic agreements about life after death.

1. *Every human being has a living soul that survives death.*

2. *The soul is divine and after death desires to return home.*

3. *The soul is part of a Divine Life Force.*

4. *Light is a symbol and direct experience of the Divine Life Force.*

5. *Judgment or life review exists after death.*

6. *Both friendly and unfriendly forces exist in the afterlife.*

7. *Restless souls can be stuck between worlds and unable to move on.*

8. *The living can help the dead.*

The last basic agreement—*the living can help the dead*—provides a foundation for contemporary spiritual midwifery. Although every person and every death is unique, the journey is similar enough to create guidelines so that people who so choose, with loving concern and prayers, can help a departed soul move on to the light and return home.

And, those of us who are now living can enhance our lives by using practices such as clearing our negative emotions, healing our attachments and addictions, or using music and meditation to find peace within. I believe that if we *come home* now to our divine self, death will hold no fear!

Chapter Three

The Aztec Goddess

A few months after arriving in Mountainair, I worked the desert soil cultivating a garden hoping to grow roses and even cleaned out a neighbor's chicken coop to add to my compost pile. Amid my practical chores, I received a phone call from Nancy—a close friend and spiritual confidant in Oregon. She kept hearing the name "Guadalupe" and asked for my help. I vaguely remembered the name of the Mexican Virgin Mary, but had forgotten the details and promised to check further. Having traveled to Greece, Crete, Egypt, and France searching for sightings of the Black Virgin, it shocked me to find that I overlooked Guadalupe—*Queen of the Americas* known also as *Our Lady of New Mexico*—right in my own backyard.

Legend had it that on December 9, 1531, an apparition appeared to an Aztec Indian peasant named Juan Diego on Tepeyac Hill near what is present day Mexico City. This miraculous figure had dark skin and black hair like Juan Diego and spoke to him in Nahuatl, his native tongue. She instructed him to pick roses where he knew only cactus could bloom and take them in his cape to the Bishop and tell him that the Mother of God had appeared and wanted a Temple built at Tepeyac.

Juan followed her instructions and finally got an audience with the Bishop after being turned away three times. When he knelt to hand the Bishop the roses, Juan's cape fell to the ground revealing an imprinted image of the divine figure. The Bishop impressed with the dark image named it *Guadalupe* after the Dark Virgin Mary honored in Spain.

Today, almost 500 years later, that cape with Guadalupe's still vibrant image draws millions of devotees to the Basilica de Guadalupe built on that Tepeyac Hill.

This popular story is the one most told, but I also found an alternate tale. Since time immemorial, Tepeyac had been the Great Temple site of the Earth Goddess Coatlique—*She of the Serpent Skirts*, also known as *Tonantzin*—Our Revered Mother. Tonantzin, the great creator and destroyer, brings us into earthly life and receives us back at death. Ten years before her appearance to the Indian peasant, Cortez had destroyed Tonantzin's Aztec shrine.

From the moment the Catholics landed in Mexico, they tried to force their beliefs on the indigenous people, but the Aztecs simply would not convert. According to *The Aztec Virgin* by John Mini, the Aztec people were inseparable from their spirituality. To leave their faith behind would mean to give up their very identity as humans.

The Catholic mission aimed to destroy the Aztec culture including the people who refused to accept the Catholic god. The war continued for ten long years as the land ran red with Aztec blood. Then Tonantzin appeared to the Aztec peasant and her devotees flocked to the temple built on Tepeyac to worship Our Lady of Guadalupe.

How fascinating, I thought. *This apparition, calling herself the Mother of God in a form that looked like Virgin Mary, appeared on the very spot where Tonantzin had been worshiped. The Aztec Mother God returned to save her people. Guadalupe, like so many previous ancient goddesses, had remanifested and found her way into this organized religion.* I grew roses in my garden where before only cactus bloomed and thanked Nancy for asking about Guadalupe.

Later, the Albuquerque Museum of Art and History hosted the exhibit *The Road to Aztlan: Art From a Mythic Homeland*. I discovered that the Aztecs believed that Aztlan was their mythic homeland where their ancestors lived in an earthy paradise. In the twelfth century they moved south to central Mexico on a migration that lasted several generations. According to ancient legend, Aztlan was located somewhere in the American Southwest.

This discovery helped me understand why Our Lady Guadalupe, who bridged the gap between the ancient Aztecs and their descendents, also played an important role in the daily lives of the people in the Southwest. For over 300 years, according to the book *Guadalupe—Our Lady of New Mexico,* she had been honored by these people as their spiritual mother. Guadalupe's name appears everywhere and her image graces tombstones, prayer cards, street murals, and folk art. Feasts and plays are held in her name and many pilgrimages are undertaken annually by her devotees.

Wanting to know more about this Dark Virgin, I chose to join one of New Mexico's largest and oldest pilgrimages to Guadalupe in Tortugas, a village near Las Cruces. On December 9, 2001 I wrote in my journal: "Tomorrow the pilgrimage begins. I go with humble heart, eager to meet the Dark Virgin, to walk and talk with Our Lady whom the pilgrims call their 'invisible companion.'"

The evening ceremony began December 10th at the Casa de Pueblo with an all night vigil. An honor guard of costumed men sang and danced the image of Guadalupe into the hall on a hand borne float surrounded in plastic flowers. All night long devotees walked or crawled on their knees to her alter, lighting candles and offering prayers. They recited the Rosary accompanied by shotgun blasts to frighten off evil spirits. Most of the participants greeted one another and chatted, I sat silently alone. Although I appeared as an outsider to others, the Dark Virgin knew no strangers.

The next day at 5:00 AM a procession of pilgrims singing morning songs accompanied Our Lady from the Casa de Pueblo three blocks to the Nuestra Señora de Guadalupe Church where the devotees gathered to ask Our Lady's blessing. Forming a circle in the parking lot, a Native American leader called in the four directions. Then the procession moved across and under two freeways, where the leader had to stop traffic. The cortege, some singing and others praying, moved along the four-mile trek through sand, dirt and brush to the base of the Tortugas Mountain where we gratefully rested and used the outhouses. Then the pilgrims, at their own pace, made their way up the steep mountain path in a freezing rain where later the priest (who came in a car) celebrated a mass.

In the afternoon, lying in bed at the Motel 6, I reminisced—*This old pilgrim fell behind to the back of the line where even a few stragglers walking barefoot passed me by, but I made it to the top. I lit a candle, ate my dry lunch amid families who had brought barbecues, skipped the mass and limped back down the hill shivering in the cold to wait for a hitched ride in the back of an old pickup truck. I'm exhausted!*

On December 12, Guadalupe's Feast Day, outside the church Native Americans danced and chanted with the beat of the drum paying homage to the Mother of God who appeared on Tepeyac to a humble Aztec peasant. Guadalupe/Tonantzin saved a nation almost 500 years ago and today continued to hear the prayers of her children. The 9:00 AM mass overflowed and I stood for two hours while the Bishop, priests, pilgrims and parishioners honored Our Lady amid a profusion of red roses. The Bishop cautioned the congregation not to think of Guadalupe as a goddess, but the fact he had to issue a warning made me smile. The celebration of Our Lady included Native American song and dance, a procession of the children, prayers and gratitude by her devotees and a sermon, followed by service of the Eucharist and then a feast of food. During the pilgrimage I had hoped for a personal visitation from the Dark Virgin, but to my disappointment, she remained my *invisible companion.*

About this time, three years after our move to New Mexico, I felt my purpose fulfilled. My husband and I agreed to move back to Oregon. Before we left, I made one last visit to Chimayo—an old abode mission northeast of Santa Fe, believed to be built on sacred earth with miraculous healing powers. The ashes of my friend Kurt, the neighbor who died with AIDS, rested there in the courtyard. I came to say good-bye and brought home a bit of the sacred dirt and a bottle of Holy Water.

Driving down a gravel road a few miles from my house, I saw something moving on the ground in front of my car, but too late to stop. After passing over the spot, I glanced in the rearview mirror and saw a cloud of dust and an object that looked like a piece of rope thrown in the air. *Oh, my god!* I gasped. *What did I hit?* Stopping the car, I got out and went back to look at the damage and spied a motionless snake lying in the dirt. I felt terrible. Here I was returning from a healing pilgrimage and ended up killing a snake—a hallowed symbol to many ancient goddesses. The shedding of the snake's skin represents the transmutation of the life-death-rebirth cycle. I ran back to the car to grab the Holy Water and then sprinkled it on the inert creature lying in the dirt. It curled up and rattled! I jumped! The snake then slithered across the road and into the brush.

Did I kill the snake and restore it to life or was it just stunned and then revived by the water? Did I save its life or did it choose not to take mine? Maybe, just maybe, as I prepared to leave New Mexico, I finally had my encounter with Coatlique—the Earth Mother—She of the Serpent Skirts—known to the Aztecs as Tonantzin, the Creator and Destroyer Mother Goddess, whom a bishop named Guadalupe.

Chapter Four

The Rocks Cry Out

In the spring of 2002 we left the stark beauty of the Southwest desert accompanied by Wolf—our dog, The Queen—our cat and two new kittens. Our other cats, Guy Kitty and B.C., sorely missed, lay buried in the adobe earth and the goats had found new homes. We returned to the green mountains of Oregon and realized each landscape held its own charm. The dreams of departed souls had stopped and somehow so did my desire to play the harp. Our family welcomed us home, but personally I felt adrift; I still had not found *my* Aztlan—my mythic homeland.

After a period of restlessness, not knowing what to do next, I renewed a previous relationship with an associate—an elder law attorney. Before moving to New Mexico I had worked as a Professional Guardian and Conservator, a practice begun in California in the late 1980s. It involved my appointment by the Court to make medical, health and/or financial decisions on behalf of an incapacitated person. This practice allowed me to use my experience as a nurse and counselor and spiritual midwife and gave me great emotional satisfaction, but my spirit still stirred and felt unfulfilled.

My continued encounters with the goddesses especially with Guadalupe/Tonantzin, who I met in New Mexico, encouraged me to continue my pursuit with the Sacred Feminine. I wanted more. My soul desired to commune with the World Soul. I decided to write and struggled with the words to describe my feelings. My attempts to connect filled pages, but I heard no response in return. Who speaks for the Earth Mother and the World Soul? Unable to hear her voice in organized or in unorganized religion, in meditation, in literature or in other peoples' experience, I continued to seek a personal encounter.

About this time Dan Brown's blockbuster *The Da Vinci Code* hit the newsstands. Recognizing many similarities with my own previous research, I pulled out my old manuscript on Joan of Arc. Having written of her relationship with Mary Magdalene and the Priory of Sion, I felt encouraged to try and ride *The Da Vinci* coattails and reedited my book.

In an attempt to find a publisher, I sent out query letters and two agents responded. Copies of the manuscript flew off to New York and I headed for a Writer's Conference in Maui. While I attended the meeting, Mitch read over the manuscript. He found pages missing in the chapter about the Black Virgin of Le Puy—the place Joan sent her mother on pilgrimage before her battle at Orleans. When rewriting I'd added this chapter and *Googled* the Internet for a description of Le Puy.

The missing pages could have been due to an errant copy machine, but I thought it more likely a message from the universe—*You can't get away with writing about a place you've never been.* The universe doesn't let me get away with much. I knew this omission needed correction and called for bold action. I surprised Mitch by telling him the missing pages meant I had to fly off to France and visit the Cathedral of Notre Dame du Le Puy. He just shook his head, he knew better than argue with my intuition.

Following are some journal entries from that excursion:

"Le Puy, October 30, 2004—8:00 P.M.

After a long and tiring trip, I finally arrived in this out of the way place surrounded by mountains in south central France. The yeasty scent of the bread from the *boulangerie*, the heady taste of the wine and many cheeses, the narrow streets and brightly colored flowers of the sidewalk vendors, all welcomed me. *Merci!*

"I'm staying at a small hotel within walking distance of the Cathedral of the Black Virgin. Tomorrow I'll make the pilgrimage. Tonight

I'm having a glass of Saint Emilion and some Camembert cheese, and of course a baguette. Luckily I found a market right next to the hotel and I'm eating in. After a hot bath, I'll relax, get some needed sleep and maybe a dream. Ah, the night before Hallowed Eve, the veil should be thin between worlds.

"4:00 A.M. ... Woke up with a dream voice ringing in my ears—'There is no Enneagram!' Wow! Will my spiritual teacher be surprised. She believes that the Enneagram of Types, based on nine distinct personalities explores an ancient system for self-understanding. In the parlance of the Enneagram, the *seven* accurately pegged me as the joyful enthusiast, a busy, fun-loving optimistic person with a spontaneous and scattered nature. In the dream I replied, 'I know, that person I thought I was does not exist. It's all a cover for the fact that I am a zero, have to pretend I am a seven.' I lay awake wondering what the Enneagram had to do with this trip.

"October 31—8:00 A.M. ... I left the hotel and walked on cobblestone streets up the hill to the Cathedral and stooped to pick up a gray and white feather on the road. I listened and looked, but did not see a bird. Along the way I noticed a niche in the outside of an ancient brick house holding a seated, small, weathered statue of the Black Virgin; she looked so forlorn. I kept walking. As I approached the Cathedral steps, a black cat crossed my path. 'Bon Jour, Madame Bast,' I saluted. The cat stopped, turned and stared at me with stealthy green eyes, then nonchalantly sauntered away. The Egyptian Cat Goddess Bast, Egypt's most sacred animal, is a goddess of music, sexuality, pleasure and life-embracing feminine fertility. I love cats. What a way to start the day: the gift of a feather at my feet, a wise weathered face guiding the way and a black sacred cat crossing my path. I climbed the stairs to the Cathedral.

"8:30 A.M. ... I pushed open a heavy wooden door and quietly stepped into the darkened sanctuary and stopped short. A statue of Joan of Arc in full armor with sword in hand stood nearby. Surprised, I bowed in greeting then anxiously turned and looked at the altar to see the famous Black Virgin—my heart sank. Twenty-seven inches tall, she seemed almost lost buried under a coat of brocade and jewels and resembled some kind of doll. Disappointed, I asked myself:

Where is the mystery? Something was missing. I knew the people of Le Puy loved her. Her banner had led the crusades, she had drawn millions of devotees to this site, I did not understand. Had I made a mistake? Then, I remembered this stone doll-like figure was *not* the Black Virgin that prompted Joan to send her mother on pilgrimage. The revolutionaries had pillaged and burned *that* Black Virgin, a cedar statue. I recalled it was a black burial stone that healed the widow. Oh my god, that fits with the message of the dream—*I am not a seven, but a zero—a no thing.* And, the Black Virgin is *not* this gilded marble figurine, *or* a cedar statue, *or* a black rock. She is not any *one* thing, but a *no thing*—a 0, a round circle that contains every thing—an ancient symbol of the Feminine.

"9:00 A.M. … I sat alone in the Cathedral. The mass would begin later. I felt fortunate to have the place to myself and went back to Joan's statue. 'Oh my friend, what's going on? I came all this way to be inspired by the Black Virgin and all I see is a fancy doll. Remember when you spoke to me twelve years ago on another Hallowed Eve? You told me, *Do not write about what I did, but who I am.* I finished your book, but did not do you justice—I still don't know *who* you are.'

"A voice answered—' I am *not* the mortal body that they burned—that vessel held my spirit. The Black Virgin is *not* the wooden image that they burned—that vessel held her spirit. The vessel vanishes, but the spirit remains. The messenger dies, but the message lives on. Write about that.'

"9:30 A.M. … I walked quietly across the Cathedral and sat by the ancient Fever Stone that healed the sick widow. A Crucifix hung above the black slab of burial stone, giving it the appearance of an empty sarcophagus. Votive candles flickered. I wondered if they burned for the crucified figure or for the healing stone. 'Please help me,' I pleaded to the Sacred Feminine Spirit, honored on this hallowed ground since ancient times.

"'I am nowhere and everywhere,' a voice responded. 'Continue your journey. This stone holds my spirit, but look around you. I am in every rock and if you do not speak, the very rocks will cry out my name.'

"I knew then that the flickering candles burned for me."

"Nothing is as it seems or as I imagined," I told Mitch at the airport when he picked me up. "I followed the call of the Black Virgin all the way to Le Puy and discovered her spirit inhabits the rocks in my own back yard."

He nodded knowingly. "I could have told you that."

I rewrote the chapter about Joan's mother and the pilgrimage and sent it off to the agent with apologies for the former mishap. Now I had another pursuit. At some point in time I needed to reconcile the meaning of the three messages I received in Le Puy. The meaning of the dream—*I am not a 7, but a 0;* the meaning of Joan's words—*the messenger dies, but the message lives on. Write about that;* and the meaning of the admonition I received from the stone—*if you do not speak, the very rocks will cry out my name.*

Chapter Five

My Mother/Myself

Over the next year I pursued publishing my book *The Joan of Arc Legacy*, but apparently Dan Brown's coattails weren't long enough. In May of 2006, an advertisement on the Internet intrigued me—*On the Footsteps of Mary Magdalene in France—a Journey on the Search for the Sacred Feminine. France is the country where Mary Magdalene arrived after the Crucifixion and where she lived until her death. We will be visiting sites that have to do with her history in France… and also sites that honor the Black Madonna (she is Mary Magdalene!).*

It surprised me that someone else connected Mary Magdalene and the Black Madonna. I joined the journey. Walking in Mary Magdalene's footsteps opened my heart to the sorrow and compassion of this woman. We ended our nine-day pilgrimage in Paris at the same time *The Da Vinci Code* movie debuted and continued our search in the unfolding mystery of Mary Magdalene and the Sacred Feminine.

Before returning home, I traveled alone to pay homage to the Black Madonna of Czestochowa known as the Queen of Poland. Her scarred face spoke to me of my own wounds. Her spirit that inspired revolutionary forces opposing oppression inspired me as well—another Black Madonna, another face of sorrow and compassion.

Upon my return from Europe, Mitch reported that my mother had been admitted to Hospice with congestive heart failure and did not have long to live. Exhausted from the trip, but panicked with the news, I immediately left for her bedside.

Crowned by her henna colored hair and demanding lipstick, my mother continued to suck life from all those around her and had commandeered a committee. At age 92, near death and on comfort care only in the hospital, she struggled against dying. Daughters, granddaughters, hospice social workers, varied medical personnel, three chaplains and assorted extended family and friends tried to help and accompany her down that final road. In the end, life had disappointed her. Her dried up body that once attracted men as bees to the honey pot, the beauty, the youth, the sex, all had withered. Her secrets, her deceptions, the abandonment of her children ate at her soul. Unable to accept forgiveness from her Baptist God, who dealt in rewards and punishments, she feared her Judgment Day and clung desperately both to myself and my sister pleading—"Don't leave me alone! Don't forsake me!"

At an early age my mother ran away from her Tennessee hillbilly home, ventured to the City of the Angels, married, divorced, aborted one child and panicked at being pregnant again—all by the age of 18. Abandoned by her lover, she struggled alone, and in her womb I waited. I believe my mother and I made an agreement—she would give me birth in this life and, upon her death, I would help her restless soul find peace. We now faced that moment, but she couldn't let go. I had helped my brother die, but couldn't help her. I sat for a week at her bedside until a sharp pain around my heart made me fear for my own well being. Then I said my good-byes and returned home, but closure eluded us both. She died a month later, fighting bitterly to the end—the day after my 74th birthday.

I didn't attend the funeral and felt no grief, good or bad, only relief. The connection had been severed long ago. Over the years, the plight of departed restless souls had stirred my imagination. I knew the living could help the dead, but before assisting my mother in the *afterlife*, I needed to deal with her legacy to me in this life. I wrote in my journal.

"My Mother's Legacy: What I know about sex, I learned from that beautiful red-haired Aphrodite. She flirted, played with life, sang, danced on tables in a daze of alcohol, and loved her way through World War II and beyond. Amid one-night stands, five marriages and two more children, she ignored the effect on this budding teenage daughter who she introduced as her sister. I only wanted a normal mother in an apron and not a Rita Hayworth. She embarrassed me.

"I turned to the church, signed pledges to never drink or dance and looked to the Father, Son, and Holy Ghost for deliverance. I longed to create my own family and be a good mother. At seventeen, I married the first boy who asked. At 23, with three children, God and a husband in tow, I thought my world complete, then I went to college. That academic path led me into a new world, away from my staid husband and family. Attracted by the glamour of education and recognition, I left the church, started drinking, dancing on tables and became my mother.

"Now I wonder what ties bind mothers and daughters and do they hold beyond the grave? Can my mother's death allow me to break some of the old emotional and sexual attachments? I don't want to hear another person sympathize, 'I'm so sorry your mother died.' I need to get away, out of my normal environment, and the reach of 'well meaning' friends."

A workshop advertisement popped up in my e-mail…

EMBODY YOUR ECSTASY! THE INITIATION FOR WOMEN

Have you "made it" on many other levels, but are missing intimacy, love, connectedness? Do you love sex, but feel you are missing something? Is your Shakti, your spiritual-sexual energy alive? How does the Divine express itself through the passionate woman in you?

Intrigued, but not sure what that all meant, I knew that the experience would take me out of my *normal* environment and shake up my *Shakti*—my idea of sexual energy was anything but spiritual. Ready to experience the Divine Feminine energy within myself, I signed up.

Sacred Sexual Initiation

Caroline and Joan, two teachers from Hawaii, guided the Spiritual Sexual Initiation into the Divine Feminine Mysteries. We gathered together for three days at a private, beautifully wooded retreat center near Portland, Oregon. The teachers compared the woman's body to the temple of the Goddess and the *sacred spot* as the key to the fountain of our feminine creative energy. During the weekend we would all have a chance to experience the initiation—the awakening of that sacred spot.

Yikes! I thought. We're going to do what? My flabby thighs quivered. Oh my god, what have I gotten myself into?

We met in a room artfully decorated with flowers, soft music, lighted candles and the scent of fragrant oils. A group of 24 women of all ages, stages and sizes, sat expectantly in the buff, trying to divert our eyes from each other. Several of the younger women spoke of my bravery (well, I hoped this aging Aphrodite wasn't too old for the *awakening*). After introductions, discussion, partner yoga and a demonstration, we divided into triads for our own *personal* experience.

Before my mind changed, I quickly offered myself as the first recipient—a sacrificial lamb. Lying down on a comfortable mat, a beautiful ample-bodied, 40 something, professional massage therapist named Marsha touched me gently. The second woman in the triad, Gloria, a fair-haired, thin mid-age woman, shyly supplied the oils and unguents. Marsha's hands moved slowly, gliding, pulsing, circling, and spreading sensuous warmth throughout my body.

My soul heard the words *wise and beautiful woman* as I bathed in that luxurious moment. Then, after being helped into a sitting position, I sat sandwiched between the two naked soft female bodies, like jam between two pieces of fresh warm bread. We rocked. It felt transforming to accept this non-threatening loving touch between women without a sexual connotation.

Later, my chance to be the "hands on" *initiator* arrived. I sat with my legs outstretched on the floor while Gloria lay flat on her back facing me, her extended legs lapped over mine. Her pale skin stretched tightly over her thin body—a dark ugly scar replaced her left breast. Surprisingly, I felt totally comfortable seeing this grown nude woman lying between my legs as if I had birthed her. Looking at her uneasy face, I asked what she hoped to receive from this initiation. Her anxious eyes darted swiftly around the room and finally came back to mine. "Healing," she replied and hesitantly added, "I only loved once when I was a teenager, and oh, by the way—I'm not afraid."

Drawing on my experiences, I surrounded this woman with light and compassion. Marsha poured massaging oil into my nervous hands and I rubbed them together. "May I touch your body? Is it tender around your scar?" I asked for permission and direction.

Looking tense, Gloria nodded her assent, but told me not touch the scar. I honored her wishes and carefully began to stroke her wounded body with loving hands. But as the energy pulsed through Gloria, her nerves reacted in fear at the strange sensation of another's touch. A cry rose up from deep inside and her arms flailed, Marsha moved quickly and held her. When Gloria relaxed I continued to administer the rites of healing—the sacred acts of love. Then the fear returned, her eyes flashed like a startled deer and her chest heaved. "My back," she moaned. I reached my strong hands under her and supported her back, caressing it with my fingertips.

Joan, one of the teachers, came over and knelt beside us, placing her hand gently on Gloria's heart and tenderly gazed into her eyes. We all poured our loving energy through our fingertips into this frightened and wounded soul. She relaxed and then in a moment submitted. As Gloria lay back down, she asked me to continue.

Then her eyes expressed disappointment. "I don't feel anything," she said. "I've been numb all my life. Why can't I feel anything?" Tears slid down her cheeks.

A visual image came to my mind's eye of a slowly melting block of ice. I shared the image with Gloria and she agreed. "Yes, I can see that too."

This is a process not an event, I remembered. Then I gently lowered my body onto hers. We touched at all points (a new experience for me) as I whispered comforting words into her ear.

"I feel the ice breaking," she murmured. "I feel the healing."

I, too, felt a healing. I, too, felt a melting and breaking of old emotional blocks.

Later, I wrote in my journal: "My life path led me to that Initiation—to the healing power of the setting and the group, to witness transforming sexual energy into sacred ritual. I became the daughter, the mother, and the crone. That moment opened my eyes and allowed me to see, to understand my mother's life, forgive her, and myself, and grieve her death. Out of my awakening flowed the divine feminine ability to heal another and to be healed. In her lifetime my mother did not know the sexual as sacred or experience this personal healing. But—the living *can* help the dead—the daughter *can* give life to the mother."

Chapter Six

After Death Communication

Serendipity—making fortunate discoveries accidentally—always played an important part in my life. In the summer of 2006, after I attended the Sacred Sexual Initiation, my friend Carolyn called asking, "Have you heard of Ervin Laszlo? He is a brilliant professor of philosophy and systems theory, a prolific author, nominated twice for the Nobel Peace Prize, and he speaks our language."

"No, I've never heard of him." I answered. Carolyn is brilliant in her own right and often grasps ideas that send me spinning, but I love the challenge. "What does he write about?"

"He combines nature, life, consciousness and the Akashic Field."

"Is that the same as the Akashic Records that are suppose to hold everything that ever happened?" I asked.

"Akasha is the all-encompassing field that underlies everything," she answered. "He writes about how physical reality and spiritual reality are two faces of one whole."

"That's not new," I said.

"Of course he realizes it is not a discovery but a *re*-discovery of a very old insight. I think you'll enjoy his vision. Look him up and let me know what you think." Serendipity.

Always on the lookout for other people's verification of my own personal experiences, I found his latest book *Science and the Reenchant-*

ment of the Cosmos—the Rise of the Integral Vision of Reality. My eyes lit up when reading Laszlo's discussion of immortality. He mentioned several forms of after death communication including those I knew such as Raymond Moody's "Near Death Experiences," mediums, and others who had made contact with the deceased or the deceased had made contact with them.

One therapy new to me caught me eye and I started making notes to myself. "Laszlo mentions on page 74 that Allan Botkin, an experienced psychotherapist has induced after-death communications, which he calls IADC, in over three thousand patients. Dr. Botkin and his colleagues hear their patients describe communication with the deceased person, hear them insist that their reconnection is real and watch repeatedly as the patient moves almost instantly from an emotional state of grieving to a state of relief and elation. The therapist produces an altered state of consciousness by means of a series of rapid eye movements known as 'sensory desensitization and reprocess.' It allows people to open their ordinary state of consciousness to extraordinary impressions. Botkin believes from his experiences that individual consciousness *does* survive death."

Realizing this stuff was right up my alley, I ordered Botkin's book *Induced After Death Communication: A New Therapy for Healing Grief and Trauma*—another serendipity.

Becky excitedly described to me what she experienced. "I saw my mother," she said, a broad smile across her tear-stained face. "I told her, 'I love you,' and she said, 'I love you too.' Then she hugged me. I could actually feel her arms around me…I've been an atheist my whole life," she said, "but I'm sure now there really is life after death." At the time of this experience, Becky's mother had been dead for five years.

This story begins Botkin's book and in the end he concludes—"It is the experience of *reconnection* that heals," referring to the after death communication.

After finishing his book, I realized Botkin's experiences paralleled my own. When I met departed souls unable to move on, I *connected* with them and that connection helped bring healing and release. I wondered if the altered state of consciousness produced by the rapid eye movement was similar to the shamanic journey and another way to walk between worlds? Calling Dr. Botkin, I asked his opinion. He kindly suggested that I might be the only person who could answer that question because he was a *simple Midwest* psychologist who knew nothing of shamanism or walking between worlds.

Dr. Botkin offered training to other therapists. I decided to sign up and learn how he induced after death communication. But before the training I wanted to personally experience his IADC process for myself and made an appointment at his Center for Grief and Traumatic Loss in Libertyville, Illinois.

On a brisk Saturday morning in October 2007, I met with Dr. Botkin in an otherwise empty office building on the first of my two-day IADC sessions. Day one involved preparation for the *after death communication* planned for day two. He shared with me how he stumbled on this procedure when working over twenty years at a Veterans Hospital near Chicago. He explained that many of the veterans suffered from post-traumatic stress disorder. Dr. Botkin often used the Eye Movement Desensitization and Reprocessing for treatment, which involves a specific set of eye movements while a client attends to a disturbing occurrence. After a number of eye movement sets the disturbing occurrence is usually fully accessed, desensitized and reprocessed. Clients typically report psychological breakthroughs that normally would take months to achieve.

"With my veterans," Al explained, (now on a first name basis) "I found most of them had a *core of grief,* a profound sadness covered by guilt or anger. I *accidentally* discovered that in the eye movement process some of my clients could communicate both visually and verbally with the departed person connected to their core of grief. I can't explain it, but the departed spirits impart information relieving the guilt or anger that the client has carried for years—it becomes a healing encounter." Al continued, "When I shared these experiences with colleagues, they began to replicate my positive results with their own clients. Later in my private practice, I offered these services to the general public. Now it's your turn. Tell me about the person you want to contact."

"My mother died this past July," I replied. "I don't feel much sadness, we had a difficult relationship. I remember at about the age of three, standing in a crib holding up my arms crying, 'up, up,' hoping someone would come, but no one came. I found out later that my mother had left me with my aunt and taken my baby brother to visit family in Tennessee. I felt abandoned. Another time about the age of thirteen," I continued, "she left me again and went to Tennessee to have a baby, but kept her pregnancy secret. I didn't know until I went to visit and saw her nursing the baby. My mother said, 'This is your sister.' I felt betrayed and very angry. We had never been close and that made it worse."

"The baby in the crib sounds more like an inner child issue." Al said. "You know that you can pick up that abandoned child yourself and give her all the love and attention she needs. Do you know about Inner Child work?"

"Well of course, I'm a therapist," I felt defensive. "I've conducted many workshops for women helping them find what I call *The Daughter Within.*" Then a sense of embarrassment washed over me remembering all the years I'd lived with the pain of that abandoned child in the crib and never thought to pick her up myself.

"Before we do anything else I think we had better do some eye movement and let you rescue that child." Al said.

So we did. Al demonstrated the EMDR process—he waved a wand back and forth in front of my face. Holding my head still, I followed the wand back and forth, back and forth, with my eyes. Each set lasted about thirty seconds, then I closed my physical eyes and reported what I *saw* in my mind's eye. EMDR is not hypnotism, I stayed very conscious and the process felt more like a waking dream or visual imagery. After several eye movement sets, I could *see* that crying baby with her arms held high and I picked her up and held her tight.

After the session and back in my hotel room, I sat in a chair hugging a pillow as the substitute child and infused it with years of unshed tears. In my journal I wrote—"I've rescued many of my ancestors and others in need, now I have rescued my own abandoned child. What a gift to myself."

The following day with a bouncing step, I walked into our second session. "Thank you Al, you really hit that right on. My inner child is grateful and feeling loved. It's amazing how we are so blind to our own issues. I'm ready to meet my mother."

Al knew I had needed to rescue my own inner child stuck in the crib before going to the next step. "Well then," he said, " I think we're ready to move on." He picked up the wand.

I tried to form a picture of my mother as we started the eye movements. It took several sets before an image flashed in my mind. I saw a barefoot young woman in her late teens with long red hair, dressed in a simple cotton frock, carrying a baby. I recognized her as my mother. She approached me and said in a gentle way, "You are strong and you'll be fine." Then she turned and walked down a dirt road holding the child. I knew she had work to do.

The Johnny Cash song—*A Boy Named Sue* came to mind. The song is about a father leaving his baby son and giving him the name "Sue" because he knew the boy would grow up tough defending himself from ridicule. Somehow I felt my mother's early disconnection had also left me to fend for myself. A hard way to grow up, but yes, I ended up strong. Now my mother had another chance to try it again. At first I thought the child she held in her arms could be the baby she had aborted before I was born. But on reflection I believe that child in her arms was me.

Is it possible to go back in time and change our past? And, if that happens, then does it change the present? Laszlo claims that evidence from cutting-edge sciences shows there is a cosmic memory field that contains all information—past, present, and future. Studying ancient traditions I found a strong belief that the living can help the dead.

Now I asked myself can the dead, by their actions in the *afterlife*, help the living? Possibly my mother was able to do things for me now that she was psychologically incapable of doing in her lifetime. If that is true, her death and work on the otherside could help heal the old wounds inflicted before my birth—could assuage the feelings of being afraid, ashamed and alone. This induced after death communication experience raised a lot more issues than it solved. I had expected that my mother would apologize and feel remorse for her behavior. Instead I observed in our reconnection that she still had work to do, and so did I—we both had a second chance to love a child.

Chapter Seven

A New Way To See

"Are you disappointed?" My husband asked. Mitch sat with a cup of tea in his big comfortable chair—his jowls sagged. Returning from Chicago, it alarmed me to note how he seemed to age when I didn't see him, even for awhile. We discussed my after death communication with my mother.

I sipped my tea, "Yes and no," I said, feeling tired from the trip. "Strolling back to my hotel after the final session, I thought *that's just like my mother to avoid confrontation and walk away—she did it to me again.* But on refection I believe she did the best she could, at least what she thought best at the time. As a naïve farm girl, my mother looked for adventure in the big city and met reality instead and I got caught in the middle. When I *saw* that young country girl, I knew that Al was right— the experience of reconnection heals. It didn't change the outcome, she still wasn't there when I needed her, but the sting of resentment and anger disappeared. That's how EMDR works."

"What does that mean?" Mitch asked.

"Well, EMDR stands for Eye Movement Desensitization and Re-processing, it's based on the theory that the brain heals naturally, just like the body. And, just like the body, it sometimes needs help to heal. A traumatic memory causing stress, guilt or fear can get 'stuck' in the brain and requires assistance to move on. The brain separates two forms of memory—short-term memory holds current emotions—long-term memory holds less of an emotional charge, it's more like watching a movie. EMDR uses the metaphor of a train moving a traumatic event from short-term memory across the brain to long-term memory where feelings dissipate. People like the tragic veterans with post-traumatic stress disorder re-live their painful war memories over and over again. It's a living hell. This therapy really seems to help."

"So how does the brain know where to store the event?" Mitch leaned forward when I mentioned the veterans. "Does short term memory automatically move over to long term memory with time? You know they say *time heals all wounds.*"

"Usually, but the emotions aren't always resolved. Sometimes the event itself fades, but negative emotions stay on and get *triggered* when something similar happens—like my feelings of abandonment. My mother left me as a baby, the memory faded, but the feelings remained. Then later, afraid of being left again, I would leave relationships first. Not consciously of course, but that childhood memory continued its effect.

"In Al's office when I picked up that crying child in the crib and held her, it didn't change the memory, but the anger and the fear disappeared. Somehow the eye movements diffused the feelings. I don't understand it, but it works. I'm anxious to learn more and it is the basis of Al's after death communication therapy. In order to take his training, I need to attend an EMDR workshop."

"You mean you're going away again? You know I have a persistent cough and trouble bending over, I'm not sure I can feed the cats or clean their litter. What do you hope to gain from all this?" Mitch sounded hoarse and looked weary.

"You know I won't leave if you're in danger," I said. "I'm trying to find other ways to tap into the Akashic Field—that cosmic consciousness where everything exists. To me it's the place of *my* soul and *my* dreams as well as the place we call death. It is the place where I do my psychopomp and spiritual work and I'm looking for different ways to enter that sacred space. I'm fascinated by it. I know it's not your thing, honey and you don't understand, but ... ."

"I just worry about you, dear and don't want you to get hurt. Get somebody in to help with the cats. I won't stand in your way." Mitch's eyes closed and he nodded off.

In December, Mitch developed pneumonia and I canceled my EMDR workshop in Los Angeles. He recovered quickly and in February 2008, I arranged for him and the cats to be cared for then joined other therapists for a three-day EMDR training at the Seattle Hilton Hotel.

"Since its initial development in 1987, Eye Movement Desensitization and Reprocessing has found widespread acceptance by much of the clinical community." The teacher welcomed us and began to explain the history and background of this unique approach. "More than just eye movement therapy, it creates a bilateral stimulation in the brain that doesn't rely on thinking or understanding. It moves dysfunctionally stored traumatic memory from one side of the brain to the other, across the great divide. We don't know how it works, but it does and ongoing research continues to provide us with confirmation and insight."

My ears perked up when the teacher said, "The founder, Francine Shapiro, believes EMDR allows the brain to reprocess material much like what happens in Rapid Eye Movement in dream sleep."

Aha! I thought. *In the late 1980s, in my dreamwork practice I began to take clients back into their disturbing dreams and counseled them to ask for help to change the outcome. It usually worked and helped resolve the issue. That is similar to this process.*

The teacher went on to outline the next three days which included lectures and practice sessions in the eight-phase process of EMDR therapy. The students broke into small groups to practice and work with each other.

When it was my turn to be the client, my practice therapist read from her script, "When a disturbing event occurs, it can get locked in the brain with all the original feelings. EMDR seems to stimulate the information and allows the brain to reprocess the experience. It is your own brain that will be doing the healing and you are the one in control. What issue would you like to address today?"

I thought of a disturbing behavior, a feeling I wanted to reprocess. "Well," I began, "when my husband tries to tell me what to do, I get very angry. For instance when he criticizes me and tells me how to load the dishwasher, it makes me feel like a child."

"What's the worst part?" the therapist asked.

"I start yelling, all out of proportion to the situation. I feel out of control."

The therapist took me through the procedures and administered the eye movement sets as I pictured the scene in my head and felt the anger—then another set, and another, until the emotions diffused. Then the therapist asked me to remember an earlier time when I had a similar feeling—a picture flashed in my mind. "About the age of thirteen," I said, "my pregnant mother left me with my Aunt Mame and Uncle Leslie. My father came to visit, something happened and he pulled down my panties, and in front of everyone, he spanked me. I felt out of control and screamed."

"Hold that negative picture," the therapist said and again administered several eye movement sets until the emotions diminished. Then she asked, "What is the earliest time you can remember feeling this out of control?"

Another scene jumped to mind. "At about the age of seven, I was in the hospital with a badly cut knee and a nurse came to my bedside with a covered tray. 'Just the two of us are going to have hot chocolate,' she said and pulled the curtain around my bed. Instead she uncovered an enema tray. It took two other nurses to forcibly hold me down while the first nurse gave me the enema. I still remember the physical struggle." My voice started shaking, "I felt so betrayed and helpless." In recalling the scene, I re-lived it. My heart raced and I could hardly catch my breath, the adrenaline pumped through my body sending me into panic. The therapist led me through more eye movement sets until eventually I calmed down.

"What words go with that picture," the therapist asked.

"I am powerless." I responded with tears in my eyes.

"What would you like to believe about yourself now?"

"That I have choices." I answered. We completed several more eye movement sets while I reprocessed those thoughts.

During the three days the students worked with each other and the staff on different aspects of the eight-phase EMDR process. Not only were disturbing scenes diffused of negative emotions, but then positive pictures and feelings replaced them. In my case, I saw a nursing supervisor come to my rescue and reproach her staff for their reprehensible behavior. She sent them on their way and then comforted me with a real cup of hot chocolate.

Later that evening in my room, I wrote in my journal. "Although this isn't suppose to be therapy for the students, these practice sessions have opened me to new insights. This EMDR really works. I realize that the baby who felt abandoned in the crib—the child betrayed and forcibly given the enema—the teenager humiliated by her father and misled by her mother—are all parts of myself that were dishonored. At every dishonoring, a piece of my soul slipped away. This reprocessing has allowed me to retrieve those lost parts and bring them home. My original presenting problem of irrationally yelling at Mitch for trying to control my behavior and treating me like a child had little to do with him, but more of a reaction to when the child felt so powerless and violated. By recognizing and reprocessing this information, I now have choices. I can choose to laugh when Mitch tries to control me because it no longer feels demeaning.

"EMDR teaches that healing goes forward, so reprocessing the disturbing episode when I was seven years old helped heal the later similar events. I wonder if something disturbing could have happened earlier in my life that could answer other questions?"

Chapter Eight

Before Birth Communication

Emily, I need your help. I want to do an EMDR session and go back to the womb. I believe something happened at that time that has affected my whole life. I took the EMDR training and found it resolves problems faster than any other therapy I've seen. It's impressive. I want to try it again."

"I've used it for years," my friend Emily replied, "often in conjunction with other therapies, it depends on the issue. It's especially effective with post-traumatic stress disorder. By the way, how was the training in after death communication you took in Chicago?"

"It was a lot to absorb at one time," I said, "since I took it right after the EMDR training. Dr. Botkin included all the protocol and techniques for the screening and intake of clients, but I was more interested in how it compares to shamanic journeying and if I can use it to access non-ordinary reality or different states of consciousness."

"You mean rather than using it in therapy with clients?"

"Yes, more for my personal use. I'm looking for ways to contact the Sacred Feminine or the World Soul, I long for a personal connection with the Divine Mother."

"What did Dr. Botkin say about that?"

"That no one else had ever made an after death connection without a specific target of a departed person. He said I was trying something new and called me a pioneer."

"Did you try it?"

"Yes, late in the day following the training Dr. Botkin taught me how to induce a personal after death communication. I tried, but I could hardly move my weary eyes back and forth. At first nothing happened, then a light flashed and I heard the words: 'You old red rooster!' David, a recently deceased friend used to call me that, he had quite a sense of humor. That was the extent of the encounter. Dr. Botkin assured me something would come through later when I tried again. That night David appeared in my dream."

I related to Emily the following dream: *David had long gray hair and looked like a shaman. He stood on a sandy island beach offering simple but wise counsel to a man and woman in the process of divorce who were arguing about how to divide their belongings. David told them to exchange something with each other that they treasured. He explained that even when a relationship ends, it is possible to take away something of value from the experience. The woman gave a red bracelet she wore to the man, then the man took off his blue bracelet and slipped it on her wrist. They each gave something of themselves and received something in return. In that way they honored each other, themselves and the relationship.*

"That's very wise counsel," Emily said. "I'll have to remember that. What do you think it meant in the context of the after death communication you were attempting?"

"I'm not sure, something to do with giving and receiving. The timing of David's recent death seems important. I'll have to think about it." Later I realized the importance of David's wisdom.

"Then let's get started." Emily pulled her chair around to face me. "Tell me again what you want to happen in this session."

"Well, Dr. Botkin told me his clients usually have a *core sadness* that is covered by their anger and guilt. The connection made in an after death communication encounter usually occurs when the client can touch the person involved with that core sadness. I felt no sadness when my mother died and realized in order to feel a loss there must be a connection. Maybe we never bonded. Or maybe the abortion attempt severed our connection. I need to return to the time in the womb and find that beginning consciousness and explore what happened. I do believe in a Cosmic Consciousness that holds everything—the past, present and the future. If consciousness exists after death, then it must exist before birth."

"I believe that too, but have never tested it," Emily said. "So let's try. Hold that thought."

As we sat across from each other she began to tap me on one knee with her left hand, then on the other knee with her right. She did the bilateral stimulation with taps instead of waving fingers or a wand—a recognized alternative in this therapy.

My eyes moved back and forth, following the touch of the taps. After three or four sets, I began to see something floating in the shadows—a large-headed fetus-like figure attached to a cord. I sensed a conscious presence and a connection. I was back in the womb. "It's hazy," I said and described what I saw. "I feel anxious and can hear crying in the distance. Wait, something is poking at my bottom," I heard my voice say, "I won't go away. I will stay." Even more determined, I declared: "I won't die! I will survive! I have a purpose!" As the cord slowly shriveled and turned black, it severed the bond with the mother. A light appeared and surrounded the head of the figure in the womb. "The figure seems to be bringing in light," I reported to Emily. "I can no longer hear the crying."

"What *are* you feeling?" Emily asked.

"Nothing, I'm numb, especially in my belly. I've been cut off from my feelings."

"How do you want to feel?" Emily asked.

"I want to feel something, maybe I can bring in the light to the navel area where that cord withered." As Emily started taping again, my eyes began to move back and forth until seeing the light flow into the center of the fetus-like figure, I knew she would survive.

"How do you feel now?" Emily asked.

"Better," I said and wiped my eyes. "That amazing tiny seed of consciousness refused to die. When her bond with the mother was severed, she turned to the light. Oh my god! That explains a lot."

That night I wrote in my journal: "This experience in the womb is where I first struggled for survival. My port, my emotional link with my mother withered before my birth. I still feel cut off from loving feelings, maybe that is why I long to find the sacred mother. But first I must reach out to that child of light and welcome her into my life. Let her know she can trust a human being—me!"

Later, using rapid eye movement, I self induced what I called a *Before Birth Communication*. I returned to the womb to revisit that courageous seed of consciousness that refused to die. She had wrestled with the angel of death and like Jacob, came away wounded. Locked in my cells all these years, was the feeling of being unwanted. I comforted that vulnerable hidden self and told her how much I loved her and invited her home to my present conscious awareness. Then for safekeeping, I placed that spiritual seed into a little white stuffed bear that sat on my bed next to a large white stuffed seal. To me, the bear then represented that courageous wounded self who fought to live because she had purpose. She was home. I hugged and cradled that bear and kissed its nose now wet with my tears, grateful for her presence.

The next day's journal entry listed the many stops on the path that had led me to this moment. It concluded: "Yesterday with Emily, for the first time, I connected with the seed of my conscious self in the womb and witnessed her courage—she refused to die. Last night, I returned to the womb and this time retrieved that hidden self and brought her safely home. I can now leave that hurt relationship with my self that no longer serves me. And as David instructed, I will give and receive something of value from the relationship. I give back my need to search for the mother and accept the gift of this wounded child. I can now commit to a new relationship with my healing self—the child is home. We have a second chance to love. I've found the mother I sought within my own soul."

Chapter Nine

What Is Real?

I'm going to stretch your imagination—if I haven't already done so," I told Mitch one night after supper. "While writing about my before birth experience, I had the feeling that I died in the womb."

"That doesn't make sense," Mitch said. "How could you die before you were born?"

"Well, I think it's more like a *near death experience* because I came back." A chill gave me goosebumps. "I can't prove it," I said, "but how else can I explain my comfort with death and dying, except that I've been there and back and have no fear. That is typical for people who encounter death and return."

"I don't understand how you could *remember* anything in the womb, there's no consciousness," Mitch responded.

"Just a minute, let me find that book I got at the Attachment Disorder Workshop I attended last month."

"Can we have dessert while we're talking?" Mitch asked as I walked away.

"Hold that thought," I said and returned with the book "Here, look at the title."

"*The Secret Life of the Unborn Child* by Thomas Verny, M.D.," Mitch read. "It says here 'the fetus can see, hear, experience, taste and even learn *in utero*. Most profoundly he can feel.' I didn't know that. And, look at this—'The chief source of those shaping messages is the child's mother.' I guess that makes sense." He handed me back the book.

"I told you so," I said. "I remembered the feelings. After that before birth experience with Emily, I wondered myself if it wasn't just my imagination. Then a notice for this Attachment Disorder Workshop showed up in the mail. It said, 'The early beginnings for attachment, perceptions, brain development begin in the prenatal period, from conception to birth—the womb is the child's first world.'"

"Do they say there is consciousness in the womb?" Mitch asked.

"Let me read this, I quote, 'Something like consciousness exists from the very first moment of conception… though his consciousness is not as deep or complex as an adult's. He is sensitive to remarkably subtle emotional nuances.'"

"That seems pretty clear and the workshop verified my own personal experiences." I showed Mitch the book. "The teacher explained that early trauma is hard wired into the brain. That means it's hard to get rid of. "

"Well, that helps me understand why you believe in your experience. This is all new to me, but I can't argue with research. It's amazing. But didn't you think your work with death and dying had something to do with your Grandmother Mary Jo's legacy? Didn't she help people cross over?"

"Yes, back in Tennessee, she helped her farm neighbors when they died. She had *the sight*—she could see a light glow over someone's head and then saw it fade before death. She assisted souls on their journey *to* the afterlife, but to my knowledge she did not help departed souls already passed. But in my psychopomp work, I guide restless souls in the afterlife. I *know* it exists."

"Well, I'm in no hurry to find out," Mitch commented.

"I believe the world of spirit is as *real* as the physical world of senses," I tried to explain. "William Blake said, 'Man has no Body distinct from his Soul; for that called Body is a portion of Soul discerned by the five Senses.' Just think about it. What makes your soul *feel* good? It's the senses. You know how they talk about *soul food* and *soul music.* Think about those ripe peach sunsets we saw in Hawaii—a feast for the soul. Or remember how the sound of a tuneful ice cream truck perked up your ears when you were a kid—music to tickle the soul."

"You mean the Good Humor Man?" Mitch smiled. "My kids knew his route and waited by the curb."

"Yes, and the kid in me loves hot chocolate, it not only tastes good, but warms my heart as well. I love the salty smell of the ocean and the shock of the cold crashing waves—it makes me feel alive! My physical senses excite me, but the inner spiritual world excites me too."

"Yes I know, you spend a lot of time exploring those spiritual encounters of the unusual kind," Mitch laughed. "It's no wonder that your mother's husband Roy used to call you *weird.* Talking about the Good Humor Man, could we have some ice cream now?"

Mitch took his bowl of chocolate ice cream topped with a squirt of whipped crème into the den to watch TV and I took mine into the living room, ready to write.

"I believe the inner world as real as the outer one," I jotted in my journal. "Pictures seen with inner eyes and sounds heard with inner ears reveal a much larger vista—creating a vast world of possibilities. In this place the human mind expands and stretches to touch the divine and the divine mind opens to welcome the human experience. In this place the heart sees rightly and the soul finds food. In this place departed souls can communicate with the living, suffering souls can be rescued, and prayers can be heard. In this place the goddesses and gods reenact their mythologies and archetypes live. In this place dreams claim breath and come alive and visual imageries burst the boundaries of the mind. Space and time defy human logic. This place holds all memory and information—past, present and future. Here, human and divine histories co-exist and co-create. Like raindrops merging with the sea, all life unites. It is BIG! People see only a tiny part and only now and then. The outside world frowns on grownups going to this Imaginal World, but children feel right at home.

"On Saturday mornings as a child, I loved to listen to 'Let's Pretend' on the radio. Right now I can see myself getting out of bed, fixing a tray with hot chocolate and toast then carefully balancing it back to bed. Adjusting the pillows and covers, I sit and listen to fascinating fairy tales while dunking my toast, dripping with butter, into steaming cocoa and watch the bubbles of fat float on top. My imagination takes me to that magical land of princes and princesses, giants and little people, talking trees and enchanted animals, where danger lurks in the dark forest.

"My Auntie Mame and I shared the world of imagination in her small apartment on Monday nights. At 6:00 o'clock she turned the radio dial to Cecil B. DeMille's 'Lux Theater' followed by the 'Inner Sanctum' with the creaking door and 'The Shadow' who knew what evil lurked in the hearts of men. She broiled lamb chops and we ate them with pork and beans flavored with a little lamb drippings, followed by English Toffee ice cream for dessert, then topped it off with a giant 10 cent Hershey bar. I loved the world of my imagination and eating tasty food—some things don't change."

I licked my bowl of ice cream as I finished writing.

"Do you remember *The Velveteen Rabbit?*" I asked Mitch the next night after dinner. "You gave it to me a few years ago."

"I recall it very well," Mitch answered. "The rabbit asked the Skin Horse, 'What is real?'"

"Do you remember the answer?"

"I'm sure you will tell me. I see you have the book right there."

"Well after our talk last night I wanted to remind you. Here let me read. 'It doesn't happen all at once,' said the Skin Horse. 'You become. It takes a long time. That's why it doesn't often happen to people who break easily, or have sharp edges, or who have to be carefully kept.

Generally, by the time you are Real, most of your hair has been loved off, and your eyes drop out and you get loose in the joints and very shabby. But these things don't matter at all, because once you are Real you can't be ugly, except to people who don't understand.'"

"Those are comforting words to this aging rabbit," Mitch said. "I identify, especially with the 'loose in the joints' part."

"Well, I love you anyway, honey. I think that story explains what I meant yesterday. Just like beauty, reality resides within the beholder—we see with our inner eyes. The Velveteen Rabbit became real to the little boy who loved him. Some people believe you must see, hear, taste, smell or touch an object for it to be real. But I know that my visual images, my dreams, and after death encounters are as real as my five senses. Those experiences differ little from a Christian praying in a church, a Buddhist sitting in meditation or a Shaman journeying between worlds or even artists painting or poets writing."

"Some people may argue that point, especially conservative Christians," Mitch said.

"I realize that, but I believe we create our own worlds and are not limited by physical or geographical boundaries," I insisted.

"That became clear when the astronauts took the pictures of the Earth from space. It provided a whole new perspective, a different point of view," Mitch responded.

"A different point of view is exactly what I'm pursuing. Thanks for listening sweetheart. How about some dessert?"

Chapter Ten

Point Of View

My early life experiences helped form my point of view. My world view began in the womb—my first world. The lack of love and support, my mother's thoughts and feelings, along with my father's absence left their mark. Perceptions and misperceptions laid the foundation for my beliefs.

My early *perceived* reality reminds me of Plato's Cave. Plato's analogy imagines a group of people living chained in a cave all of their lives, facing a blank wall. Sometimes animals, birds, people, or other objects passed by the entrance casting shadows on the wall inside the cave. Seeing the shadows on the wall, the prisoners perceived them as real.

However, one man broke free from his chains and ran out of the cave. For the first time he saw the real world and experienced the real birds and animals and not just their shadows.

Excited, this man went back in the cave to tell his fellow prisoners of the real world out there. But to his dismay, they didn't believe him. In fact, they grew angry with him and claimed the shadows to be real and called the escaped man crazy for saying the opposite. Plato argued that the shadows represent the physical world and most people, like the prisoners in the cave, think the shadows are real.

As Plato predicted—in my early years, my world view confused what was real with the shadows. Since 1973, the years covered in these writings, my journey has expanded my worldview, but it still contains some old prejudice. Part of my ongoing work includes paying attention to other points of view.

In the fall of 2008, I attended a writing class—*The Story You Came to Tell*—at the local community college. I wrote the following paper for that class:

Point of View

"Why did you move to Mountainair?" Dick asked—the only male in the writing class who seemed quite comfortable in his role. The week before we had discussed briefly our mutual interest in New Mexico.

I told Dick, "My ancestors traveled as settlers with the Conquistadors from Mexico City in the early 1600s."

"You must be proud of your heritage, the Spaniards were so courageous and adventurous," he interjected.

"Oh no! You don't understand. I'm ashamed of the way they conquered and treated the Natives."

"But this is the way of the world," Dick's words betrayed his gentle eyes.

"It's time to start the class, I have a poem," the teacher's lyrical voice called us to attention. That ended our talk.

"He just doesn't get it," I thought to myself. "Leave it to a man to stand up for the Conquistadors. My move to New Mexico was an attempt to correct my ancestor's mistakes. Well I don't have time to explain."

In my musings I missed the point of the poem, but at the end of the class I heard the assignment—"Find four words on one page in the dictionary and write a paper."

*I awoke in the dark, my sleepy eyes squinted at the clock's red illumined numbers: **3:30**. Alert, my mind prattled like a Chatty Cathy Doll. I've never forgiven my pioneer ancestors for their role in robbing the indigenous natives of their freedom and culture. Yet, something Dick said about "how courageous they were" resounded. It bothered me that I could not forgive or forget.*

As I lay wide-awake the class assignment flashed in my mind— "four words," well I already have two of them. I got up. Locating the words **forgive** *and* **forget** *in the dictionary, I scrutinized them and their neighbors.*

Forget: not to remember. *Instead of not remembering, I choose to* **re-member** *my ancestors from a first person point of view, not in third person judgement. I want to see with their eyes, hear with their ears, feel with their hearts, and walk in their boots. "What do I feel as I struggle to homestead in a hostile new territory? What do I feel when the child in my belly quickens and I have to give birth in this wilderness so far from my mother and aunties? How do I feel when I'm told there are savages close by who would kill me or kidnap my babies? How do I cope with the lack of comfort, harsh landscape, high desert winds, the silence, the unknown, the isolation?"*

Now the word **Forgive: to pardon or remit.** *A pardoned prisoner is set free. Forgiveness means letting go of the past. By re-membering and taking my ancestors' point of view, I changed the vista—I touched the souls of my ancestors. I can now let go of my indictment. There is no one to forgive but myself. I accept the pardon. But I would suggest—the point of view of* **compassion** *is the best lens to view the world, both past and present.*

It is easy for me to condemn others and dismiss them because it makes me feel right by comparison. My early programming created in me a need to be in control for my own protection. That often led me to try and control others. It's interesting how life provides us opportunities to self-correct, if we pay attention. Let me share with you *My Summer with Sasha.*

It started with a dream of my dog Wolf. Oh, he struck a magnificent presence in the world that beautiful 125-pound independent Malamute who refused to bow his spirit or come when called. It is said of this northern breed that they are born and bred to be intelligent and strong willed with the ability to make their own decisions, coupled with an innate desire to run and a strong prey drive.

A few years had passed since his departure and the dream encouraged me to find another dog. Cruising Craig's List, I found Sasha, a 112-pound, seven-year-old Malamute mix. I transferred my love from Wolf to Sasha, but she had her own charms as well. In the house she slept by my bed and followed me around day and night.

On our walks, Sasha pulled and whined when she saw other dogs. The dog trainer called it *leash frustration*—it helped to know it had a name. One day we saw a little white dog playing off leash, Sasha jerked away and attacked the small dog as they rolled in the grass. Fortunately, the dog survived, I was a mess.

I had two dogs—Inside Sasha and Outside Sasha. Inside, I had a polite, obedient, gentle, companionable dog, good with cats and visitors. When playing with known friends, she'd be happy, running, fetching and returning. Inside Sasha was a love—Outside Sasha tried my patience.

Then one day as we walked, a man with two little dogs on leash strolled our way. In training, our homework assignment was *sitting* when other dogs passed by. So I told Sasha *sit* and with some help she sat. The two small dogs started to walk by when the little white one snarled and barked. Sasha lunged and pulled me down with her. Imagine this—*a small white dog, Sasha and me rolling around on the ground—dust flying*—and I'm no spring chicken. Gathering his two little dogs, the owner apologized and walked away leaving Sasha and me in the dirt. With tears in my eyes I looked at Sasha, beyond anger or thoughts of revenge, I knew in my heart—*I cannot keep this dog—there are things in life beyond my control.*

Sasha and I had a brief summer affair. I bathed her with fancy soap at the doggie wash, took her to school, groomed her, loved her, walked her, found friends to play, took her on car rides to visit other dogs, bought her toys, tossed her balls, laid with her in the grass and scratched behind her ears. It wasn't enough. Could her northern breed instinct be controlled? Maybe. Could I do it? No. I gave her what I could; she gave me what she could. We didn't fit—no blame, no shame. Sasha returned to her previous owner who had missed her and felt excited about having her back.

With some relief at the happy ending, I wrote in my journal: "What was that dream all about? Why a summer with Sasha at a time when I was reminiscing about my life story, ready to write a memoir? My dog Wolf brought the dream. His name came from the book *Women Who Run With the Wolves* by Clarissa Pinkola Estes. She writes, 'Within every woman there is a wild and natural creature, a powerful force, filled with good instincts. Her name is Wild Woman but she is an endangered species.' Estes claims that society tries to civilize us and silence the life-giving messages of our own souls. Sasha refused to let her wild nature be civilized, when her soul called she answered. Her innate desire to run and instinct to pull led to her leash frustration."

What a lesson. I realize that I also have a wild nature, when my soul calls I, too, feel leash frustration. I also have an Inside Jacqueline and an Outside Jacqueline who sit at opposite ends of the pole. I have my own unique instincts, hardwiring, and bloodlines.

Inside Jacqueline identifies with the Imaginal World and sees with the eyes of a child. Outside Jacqueline, a more rational thinker, lives in a civilized world and masquerades as a mature woman. Yet, we share the same body and soul.

Whether it be with my animals, myself, my family, community or country, along with others, I face at least two different ways of thinking and being in the world—different points of view. To find peace I seek reconciliation, but discover some things are beyond my control. I only have the power to make peace within my own soul.

Chapter Eleven

Remember

I just talked to Jody," I said to Mitch. (Jody is a psychic, spiritual counselor in Miami, who I consult once or twice a year.) "I wanted to check out my idea that my grandmother and Guadalupe were waiting for me rather than thinking that I moved to New Mexico to guide my grandmother's soul."

"What did she say?" Mitch asked.

"She suggested it wasn't either/or, but both. December 12, 1912, the date that my grandmother died, especially intrigued her. She thought 12-12-12 had certain significance. You know of my interest in the predictions about the Mayan Calendar that ends in December 2012 and wonder about a connection?"

"You mean the supposed end of the world?"

"No, I don't believe it is the end of the world, but certainly something important, maybe a major shift in consciousness. It's interesting that after 5,000 years, the Mayan Calendar abruptly ends on December 21, 2012."

"I feel some kind of energy shift myself," Mitch said. "I think my intuitive powers are getting stronger."

"You really helped Ann (not her real name) when you read her coffee cup on the full moon last month. She talked to me of problems with her husband, even considering a separation, but your interpretation of the situation gave her a different perspective. It is amazing what you can *see* in those coffee grounds. I can hardly see anything."

"Her husband has his own problems," Mitch said. "I'm glad it helped. Can you give me Jody's phone number? I'd like to have a reading with her. Maybe she can confirm these feelings. It's time I got more into my right brain thinking and increase my intuition. She's helped me before and I like her."

On February 24, 2009, after his phone conversation with the psychic, Mitch seemed excited, "Jody said my intuitive powers are definitely coming back. I told her I wanted to stop being so analytical and critical and be more introspective. She gave me encouragement. We talked for two hours. She really listened, called me a sage. We had a great conversation."

"I'm glad," I said. "Your intuitive side means a lot to me. Look at all the coffee readings you've done on the full moon. That information helped me write my last book."

"Jody said I should help you. I've heard that before, but I'd like to begin writing myself. She also called me a scribe."

"Well, do it honey. You won't be competing with me."

"She told me the change won't come right away, it will take a few weeks," Mitch said. "For now I need to go within and contact my spiritual source. You know meditation is hard for me, but she gave me good tips. I know it is time."

March 7, eleven days later, I was in San Diego on the first day of an International Harp Therapy Conference sitting around the hotel pool eating lunch and chatting with old friends when my cell phone rang. I flipped it open and heard the strained voice of my daughter Candace—"Mom, Mitch had a stroke. The medics are putting him in the ambulance now. I think you'd better come home right away."

"Oh my god!" I exclaimed, trying to process this news. I had just talked to Mitch two hours before at my morning break. He hadn't felt well the previous night and didn't eat dinner, but said he felt better and was fixing his breakfast. "The cats are fine and Candace is coming over soon to clean their litter," he said. "I'm okay, don't worry. I'll have my breakfast now." I promised to call him later and ended the conversation with, "I love you!"

My mind tried to focus. "What happened? Is he conscious?" I asked. "Do you know for sure?" I wanted to think it wasn't serious. I wanted to stay at the conference. I wanted life to go on as usual.

"The medics weren't sure, but said that's what it looked like. Mitch couldn't talk and his left side seemed paralyzed when they put him on the stretcher," she responded.

"I'll go to my room and call the airline and get the quickest plane home. I'll let you know when I get my reservation."

"Call my cell. I'll be at the hospital," Candace replied. "His bowl of cereal was still warm on the table, he didn't eat it. I don't think it happened too long before I arrived. He had his list of meds posted on the refrigerator and the medics knew right where to look. That was smart."

"Yes, Mitch is so organized." My mind shifted and I remembered him saying *I'm so analytical, I want to be more introspective.* I continued, "It's a miracle you came by when you did, he could have been alone there for hours." The thought made me cringe.

"I'm leaving now for the hospital. Someone will pick you up at the airport," my daughter said. "Let me know what time. I've got to go." The phone went dead. I looked around. The pool water still sparkled in the sun. People still chatted. The waiter took my salad plate. In a fog, I walked by a friend and whispered that Mitch had a stroke and I had to leave. I didn't wait for a reply.

It was midnight before I arrived at Mitch's bedside in ICU. His adult son had driven from Portland to be with his dad. Mitch had moved in and out of consciousness all day since the stroke and did not respond when I kissed him. I asked Mitch's son to tell his brother in New York and his sister in Los Angeles to come right away. Then exhausted, I went home. "Meow," the cats greeted me as I walked in the door. They were hungry.

The next day revealed the magnitude of the stroke. The x-rays showed a massive injury to the right hemisphere of the brain with total left side paralysis. The neurologist gave no hope of recovery. If he survived, and that was a question due to his age and chronic medical problems, Mitch would live out his days in a nursing home. He couldn't swallow and a technician inserted a feeding tube through his nose.

Over the next few days, every known therapist in the hospital descended on Mitch—speech, occupational, physical, inhalation, respiratory, among others. They cranked him up in a Hoyer Lift and plopped him down in a wheelchair, sat him up, poked him, pulled him, adjusted him, trying to optimize every chance for recovery. I played my harp. He drifted in and out of consciousness and wanted to go home when he was awake. He tried to communicate through his limited speech and almost illegible handwriting. Mitch did not understand that he'd had a stroke and the doctor said that wasn't unusual.

I floated in and out of my own consciousness as a nurse, counselor, spiritual midwife, harp therapist, wife, friend, confidant, advocate, guardian, conservator, and as administrator of his health care directive, I surprised myself by signing a *DNR—Do Not Resuscitate* order.

His children arrived over the next few days and Mitch rose to the occasion. He perked up when they came and even wrote a note to his son scribbling, "I love you." He signed it "Dad, Pops, Papou, and Mitcho"—all the names used by his children, his granddaughter and me. He seemed to be saying, "I love you" to each of us and maybe good-bye.

On March 16, day eight of the hospital stay, discharge plans had to be made. Mitch had not responded to any of the therapies and would no longer benefit from the intense hospital routine. He could go to a skilled nursing facility for more therapy, but considering his condition, the doctor suggested hospice—a terminal prognosis with comfort care only—time to let go. I'd been down this road many times with other people, but this was different.

Taking a long, deep breath, I gathered my strength and readied myself to bring my husband home to die. I began making arrangements. But his children had other plans. They could not let him go. This caused a great deal of conflict and opened a chasm between us, but in order to protect Mitch I acquiesced to their wishes.

On March 19, two hefty attendants transferred Mitch to a nursing facility. The staff was pleasant and smiled, saying they had lots of successes with patients like my husband. I doubted it, but smiled back. They placed Mitch in a shared room and pulled the curtain between beds. A television blared across the hall. When things settled down I played the harp as much for myself as for Mitch. This was not going to be easy. I told the staff and his kids I would give Mitch two weeks in this place and then take him home where he belonged with the cats and me.

That night, I sat at home alone looking at the sunset drinking a glass of wine and wondered what would come next. Tomorrow was the Equinox, the first day of spring and that usually meant the sign of new life, rebirth and increasing light. *Oh Mitch! What will become of us?*

The next morning, March 20, I had a caregiver conference with one of my clients in another facility and arrived to see Mitch about noon. The nurse said he had already been up in a wheel chair and did a great job. I doubted it. When I went into his room, he mumbled that they had hurt him. Upset, I marched to the nurse's station and complained. The nurse said, "Oh I'm sorry, next time we'll give him pain medication *before* we get him up." I fumed.

I went back to Mitch's room and pulled the curtain and sat at his bedside while he slept. Playing the harp, I did a cleansing of my own negative emotions before I offered the ritual to Mitch. Later, I played a CD of harp music—*Illuminations*—made to accompany a labyrinth walk. It seemed appropriate since I believe life is not an unsolvable maze, but a labyrinthine path that eventually leads back to the Center. I left at 5:00 PM and pressed the repeat button on the CD player hoping the music would comfort him and remind him of my love. Weary, I went home and early to bed.

The phone woke me up at 9:00 PM. "This is the nurse, your husband just died."

I heard myself screaming, "He died alone in a nursing home." My worst fear. I could not stop screaming.

Following is a copy of an e-mail I sent out the next day—

Dear Friends:

On Saturday March 7, Mitch had a severe stroke that left him paralyzed on the left side and unable to swallow. He survived for two weeks on a feeding tube and with attempts at rehabilitation, but from the beginning the doctor told us he would never recover and suggested Hospice. He stayed in the hospital until March 19 when he was transferred to a skilled nursing facility as his children wished for more time in hopes of recovery. Mitch passed suddenly and unexpectedly last night on March 20, the first day of Spring, peacefully in his sleep at 9 PM. I had been there all day and left at 5 PM with a CD of harp music playing "Illuminations—Labyrinthine Music." When I entered the room after his death, the music was still playing. It had carried him to the center of the labyrinth and on to his next journey. I am so grateful. I washed his body and changed his clothes and gave him lots of kisses. He did not have a wrinkle on his brow. He was at peace. We will have a service for him in Bend on Tues, March 24 and then his body will be shipped to New York to be interred next to his father and sister. I know you will join me in a toast to the Great Greek and remember him as the wonderful man he was and still is. I am supported by my family and friends and am grateful for their love.

May the Father/Mother God bless us all.

We honored and blessed Mitch at home then sent him on to New York. On March 27, after a Greek Orthodox service, he was laid to rest. A bugle sounded taps honoring this World War II veteran. The honor guard folded the American flag that draped his coffin and presented it to me.

Afterwards, I slept twelve hours a day. It took several weeks before I could write, but I knew I had to finish my book and that Mitch would help me.

Sometime while Mitch was in the hospital, I listened to the recorded tapes of his psychic counseling session with Jody, made shortly before his stroke. I heard her voice on the tape telling Mitch he was highly intuitive and a mystic, but also a caretaker and nurturing. He was a deep thinker with an active analytical mind set. I heard Mitch's voice explain that his left-brain thinking had helped him in his career and to provide for his family, he had even earned a Ph.D. in rehabilitation psychology, but now he wanted to change.

"You are a spiritual being having a human experience," Jody confirmed. "You have worked in the world with the worst of them and have been the best of them. And now it is time to surrender and let go of your attachment to the physical world. Are you willing to let go of your thinking mind and awaken to your true self, to an elevated state of new frequency, birthing your divine true nature?" She asked.

"That sounds exciting," Mitch responded. "I want to be less critical and more introspective. I want to be more spiritual like Jacqueline."

"You are a deeply spiritual person yourself and you complement each other," Jody commented. "When you complete your end of the bargain, Jacqueline will complete certain works." Jody continued by telling Mitch that he would see the light of day unfolding within weeks as a result of a clearing. By the end of March, he would have a dramatic shift in consciousness, and experience a part of his self not yet seen.

A few weeks after the funeral, Mitch's daughter and I went through his personal belongings. She found this poem. I read it for the first time.

THE PATH

The path we take at times seems difficult and unsure.
    However, it is not until we near the end of
our journey and look back down the road that we
    realize what a wonderful journey it was.

The miracle is that which we thought to be the end of
    the journey, becomes the start of a new one
down a path that we had never taken before.

Only by realizing that there is much more to being
than the brief journey that each of us takes, can
we fully know what the Divine Power has in
store for us.

The essence of our Being then takes on a larger
perspective, for we have added yet another
footprint to a well-worn path.

MJA 12/86

Mitch and I married on October 13, 1985. Did he write this poem about our new journey together or was he contemplating the larger journey of life? I'd like to think that our views about life and death were more aligned than I knew. Although I had lamented not being with him at his transition, I know some journeys must be taken alone. He chose. I honor that choice and believe our life together was part of the preparation.

Along with the poem in a notebook, I also found an old yellowed newspaper clipping of the cartoon Bloom County with Opus, the big-nosed penguin. Mitch had saved it. Opus is bidding goodbye and in each frame his size diminishes. In the first frame, a large Opus is waving and says, "Farewell, Milo! So long Lola! See you later Bill the Cat." In the second frame a little smaller Opus says "Toodle-oo Steve and Cutter John! Ta ta Portnoy, Hodge, Oliver! In the third frame, the shrinking penguin says, "Adios, Friends! Au revoir, family! Arrivederci, everyone! And in the fourth and final frame, a tiny Opus says "Good-bye me." But Opus didn't die; he lives in the hearts of everyone who remembers that funny big nosed penguin.

Mitch has said his "Good-byes," but he continues to live as long as someone remembers that Great Greek. As long as there is a Memorial Day, a Veteran's Day, his birthday or our anniversary. As long as his children remember their Dad or Pops, his granddaughter thinks of her Papou. As long as there is a full moon and a message in the grounds of a Greek coffee cup, as long as I dream, walk between worlds and write— someone remembers. Yasou Mitch!

Chapter Twelve

Reconnection

On April 9th, the first full moon after Mitch died, I went alone to Newport Beach on the Oregon coast where we often shared moments of pleasure—last time in October 2008 on our 23rd anniversary. I carried five bags of dried rose petals—Mitch loved to give me roses and I never throw rose petals away. On the sandy beach where I walked in the early morning fog, the waves broke over the rocks. I waited for the tide to go out and threw the petals into the receding waves. The wind picked them up and blew them back, which both surprised and delighted me—hundreds of red, yellow, white, peach and pink rose petals floated in the air and fell gently to the ground. A noisy cloud of gulls, dipping their wings, flew overhead and landed looking for breakfast. "Sorry seagulls," I said. "This is food for the soul—not for the body—food for the soul." The following morning, like an offering, wet rose petals spotted the shoreline and rocks. The next day they were gone, the sea had accepted my gift.

Back home on April 24th, I wanted to resume writing, but didn't know where to begin and took a stroll along the canal behind my house and asked for help. Suddenly the ideas for the next chapters fell into place—I had to write about Mitch's passing. I returned home to jot down my thoughts. In the hallway, a collage of family photographs that Mitch created had fallen to the floor—the frame still hung on the wall. He had left one empty spot at top center of the collage. I *knew* exactly the picture of Mitch that belonged in that space watching over us all. I felt his presence, the circumstances could not otherwise be explained.

April 25th, I dreamt that Mitch still needed medication, meaning he had not completely healed. In the dream I received his new meds. The next night, another dream: *My daughter Candace and another woman were visiting my home, we knew Mitch had died. We expected twenty additional women who knew nothing of his death. The women arrived and I offered them orange juice left from a Greek Easter brunch. One woman accepted and I searched for a clean glass, but could not find a single one. Mitch had used every glass and put them away dirty with pieces of pulp still stuck to the side. Each one had to be scrubbed clean. My daughter went into the bedroom and discovered the light was too dim to read, she asked that I bring in more light.* I woke up puzzled, struggling for an explanation.

Meditating on the symbols, I associated a glass with a vessel, the feminine, and the Holy Grail. An orange was round, juicy, matter—my mind jumped from matter to mater—nature, earth, and the feminine. Mitch had never forgiven his mother for betraying his father with a business partner—it broke up the family. Undoubtedly jealous of the stolen love that he felt rightfully his, Mitch told me that he could never fully trust women. All the glasses, symbols of the feminine, were dirty—bits of matter clung to the sides.

Later that day, concentrating on forgiveness, I visualized Mitch and performed a ritual to cleanse him of anger, greed, ignorance, doubt, jealousy and pride then surrounded him in abundant light and love. At the end of the ritual, I placed him in the arms of Sophia—Feminine Wisdom—the Greek Orthodox symbol of the Holy Spirit, the Comforter. That cleansing helped release him for the next stage of the journey.

Although not all traditions agree, I had learned and practiced the Tibetan Buddhist belief that a departed soul could linger in this physical realm completing unfinished business. For 42 days, I had honored and remembered departed souls—like the friends and loved ones who came into my dreams and those who died tragically or without warning. Mitch died on March 20th, the first day of spring—six weeks had passed. May 1st—May Day—Beltane, a time of celebration had arrived. The time to honor Mitch's soul and bid him farewell.

Inside our home, I had left everything in its place since the day Mitch suffered his stroke, just in case he would happen by. My friend Su, a minister of healing who officiated at Mitch's memorial service, came to the house for this ceremonial release of his soul. In the past, Mitch performed a house blessing whenever we moved to a new home. Using holy water, he touched and blessed every opening—doors, windows, fireplaces and vents—to clear the old energy and keep negative spirits away. When visiting Joan of Arc's hometown, I had brought back a bottle of water from a spring located near the Fairy Tree where it was said she had danced. I consider Joan a symbol of hope and gave Su this special water to bless all the openings, inside and out. We blessed the chairs where Mitch sat, the bed where he slept and clothes that he wore, honoring his life and freeing him to come and go as he pleased. Although to my knowledge, no other souls I released in the past had returned, I wanted to give Mitch the choice.

Next, I read a poem my daughter Candace had written as a tribute to Mitch.

> ...I remember your hands
> turning the Greek coffee cup
> around and around,
> searching for the messages,
> opening to the Muse.
>
> I remember your right hand squeezing mine,
> a rhythmic announcement,
> a Morse code,
> telling me that you were still alive after the stroke
> while your left hand lay useless at your side.
>
> I remember your hands
> both lifeless
> along with the rest of you,
> finally at peace,
> both halves reunited in stillness.
>
> I remember your hands
> holding the cross,
> reshaped in unity
> in front of the place
> where your beating heart
> joined our hearts
> during the journey of our lives together...

I read aloud the cards of sympathy and blessings that came from friends and loved ones, so Mitch could hear how they remembered him. He would appreciate that his urologist called him "a fine gentleman." Many spoke of his wisdom, wit and kindness. Su offered a personal thank you for his intuition, insight and advice and I played the *Irish Blessing of the Road* on the harp. Then in prayer, I tapped the Tibetan chime and the vibrating sounds lingered as we cleared away the pillows, no longer needed, that had propped his ailing body in his chair. "Safely Home Mitcho!" I said. "You are free to come and go as you choose." Su and I finished the ceremony by celebrating at a Mexican Restaurant with two huge margaritas—way too many spirits, but it seemed the thing to do.

On May 5th, I picked up the book, *Women Who Run With Wolves* and re-read the story of the Sealskin/Soulskin and thought of Mitch. Years before, he had made the connection for me between my dream of a harp seal and my soul that began my affair with the harp. At that moment, a smoke detector in the hallway sounded one *beep*. I said without thinking, "Mitch?" then waited to see if it would beep again, indicating low batteries, but only one beep sounded. The next morning about 3:00 AM, as I lay in bed wide awake, but not quite ready to move, the detector beeped again. I said, "Okay, Mitch. I'll get up and write," acknowledging his presence.

I wondered at the sanity of talking to smoke alarms and reread Joan Didion's memoir, *The Year of Magical Thinking*. She writes of the first year after her husband's death as a time of trying to bring him back—to undo his dying. I didn't try to bring Mitch back—he came on his own. Our spiritual connection somehow manifested in the physical realm with a falling picture and beeping smoke alarms. And yes, I changed the batteries to make sure that wasn't the issue.

On May 8th, Mother's Day, the second full moon after Mitch died, I went to Ashland to see my granddaughter dance. As I returned and walked in the door, three beeps greeted me, a welcome home. This beeping continued periodically from different detectors. One night three shrill beeps woke me up and I lay in bed frightened. Thinking it could be a warning, I got up to look around, but saw nothing amiss. "Cut it out Mitch, you're scaring me," I complained. It stopped.

Three weeks later, Mitch's daughter came to visit and sort his belongings. While we gathered his clothes, the alarm beeped three times. She heard it too and didn't doubt it was her dad communicating with us. But the beep didn't sound when Mitch's son came to help; he worried about my talking to inanimate objects.

On June 7th, the third full moon after Mitch died, I tried my hand for the first time at making a cup of specially ground Greek coffee in his mother's briki—a Greek coffee maker. Not sure of the proportions of water and sugar to the coffee, I did my best. The coffee tasted weak. At a young age, Mitch had learned to read the coffee cups from his mother. It takes a certain intuitive gift to *see* images in the coffee residue and interpret the meaning. On the full moon each month Mitch would look diligently for a message in my cup. Now I wanted to duplicate his process and sought his help.

In this ritual a question is asked, expecting the answer to be revealed in the reading. After drinking the coffee, I flipped the cup upside down on the saucer and twisted it three times clockwise, concentrating on my question and then let it set. Sitting in Mitch's chair, I turned the cup upright in anticipation and peered closely—*Would the grounds reveal their secrets to me?* I stared into the cup and only saw grounds. I waited. The cat meowed. "Get that cat out of here, I can't concentrate." I remembered hearing Mitch grumble and smiled at the image. I locked the cat in the other room and sat back down picking up the cup.

"Help me Mitch," I pleaded and peered once more into the coffee grounds. Then I saw what looked like a mountain or maybe a tree, then on closer inspection an image of a big owl emerged. Turning the cup slowly around to the other side—a dancing devil wearing a mask caught my eye. Then I made out a crane or heron with feathered wings that reached around to circle the cup joining the two symbols and also a lump at the bottom, which promised money or a message.

My question concerned my book and its meaning and two afterlife symbols appeared. An owl can see that which others cannot, the essence of true wisdom. To some American Indians, the owl is a bird of death—and the wise owl appears with witches at Halloween (the Celtic feast of the dead). The devil dancing in flames is a Christian symbol of hell. I remembered the devil killing me in one of my first visualizations many years ago, filling me with fear. The crane, a symbol of Aztlan—the spiritual homeland of the Ancient Aztecs—connected the owl and the devil. I asked myself, *Where is my spiritual homeland centered—in fear or wisdom?* These two faces of death confront us all, but the cup revealed that the devil wore a mask, he had a false face.

"Yes Mitch, with your help I'm reading the cup. Three months from the date of your stroke and the third full moon after your passing, I see a sign of wisdom from the spiritual homeland—no need to fear death, a message of hope. Thank you."

On July 7th—the fourth full moon after Mitch died—I tried my hand with a second coffee reading. I was finishing the last chapter of my book. Early on I projected it would close with the release of my Grandmother Rosella. Fate intervened. The book now concluded with the death of my great Greek warrior Miltiadis. After drinking the coffee and turning the cup upside down on the saucer, I asked the question "Is this chapter capturing the full essence of Mitch?" I remembered him sitting in silence as he stared into the cup and scowled. "Are you concentrating?" he would ask me. "I can only get out what you put in." Feeling chastised for thinking of something else, I'd quickly remember my question.

This is incredible, I now said to myself, gazing into the cup and seeing shapes revealed in the coffee grounds. *I can hardly believe my own eyes; it looks like a Rorschach test. I see the head of a bull in profile facing a dark bear coming out a cave and behind the bear a woman sitting on a camel.* Slowly turning the cup, there emerged a white-bearded sage-like figure wearing a long robe holding a lighted torch in his right hand.

The cup reinforced what I'd written about Mitch in the book's final chapter. Mitch had bull-like qualities, being born under the sign of Taurus. And, he was a bull in the marketplace and at work in his early years. The bear represented introspection and at the end of his life Mitch sought to emphasize that neglected side of his nature. Also, his daughter called him "Daddy Bear." The psychic had called him a sage. I am the woman on the camel making a pilgrimage to Egypt—a trip planned for the coming December.

That night I wrote in my journal. "Either I have suddenly acquired the gift for reading the coffee grounds or I'm seeing through Mitch's eyes. What was it the psychologist Al Botkin said when I took his training in after death communication? 'It is the experience of reconnection that heals—we need to continue a changing, dynamic relationship with the departed loved one.' Yes Al, I agree—Mitch continues to be a dynamic part of my life."

As a spiritual midwife, I've aided many departed souls trapped between worlds—souls like my ancestors, who I met on shamanic journeys in psychopomp workshops. I sought out others—like the troubled souls I met at the Vietnam Memorial Wall. Then souls of departed friends or loved ones needing assistance to drop their attachment to the physical realm began to appear in my dreams.

All these experiences helped prepare me for Mitch's transition, but our personal connection made it unique. The healing rituals—before and after his death—especially the one that gave him the choice to come and go as he pleased made the difference.

On July 16, 2009, I drove to California alone, retracing a trip Mitch and I took on our 20th anniversary in 2005. The first night I stayed with our good friend Tricia. In the early morning, I woke up startled and said aloud, "Mitch is alive!" In a dream, I saw him standing across the street and went over to greet him. "Mitch," I said, "You have been dead over three months!"

"I just woke up," he replied.

His previously gray curly hair now grew in black ringlets. On closer inspection I noticed, "You have lost all your chins!" Wide-awake in the dream, Mitch appeared youthful and renewed. *Maybe, just maybe, I thought, this life is really the dream!*

After returning home from visiting our many friends and loved ones, it disappointed me that the smoke alarm did not beep in greeting.

Was Mitch still around? With the next full moon quickly approaching, I anxiously awaited a third coffee reading.

On the afternoon of August 5th—the full moon—I brewed and sipped the Greek coffee and again sat in Mitch's chair, called on him for help, and turned the cup three times clockwise. I asked a question about how to end my book. Then scrutinizing the contents of the cup, a symbol began to emerge—a volcano shaped pillar extending from the bottom of the cup to the rim. It contained small objects that looked like flying birds. A Christ-like figure stood in a space next to the pillar separating it from the adjoining scene. Then I saw the back of a man with white hair who reminded me of Frank Morgan, the Wizard of Oz in the movie. Attempting to frighten people, he sat manipulating huge images on the wall. Scrutinizing these illusionary patterns, I saw a huge dog or a bear, a jackalope, a ghost-like figure, a winged bat and the face of a bearded terrorist. With my question still in mind I sought to interpret the message of this cup.

It seemed the scenes reflected two ways to approach death. In one, the Wizard used frightening illusionary images to alarm people about death and dying, but I saw through his deceptions. In the other, a spiritual guide stood next to a pillar providing a pathway—birds looked to be flying upwards. But on closer inspection, I noticed that the pathway allowed the figures to both come *and* go, I said out loud—*Oh, the birds do not just fly away home, but can go back and forth.* At that moment the smoke alarm sounded a startling beep—the first time since I returned home five days before.

*Oh my god Mitch, I got it! You are confirming a final message for the book—Life continues beyond death **and** after souls return to the light, they have options. They can choose to reconnect with those of us who still live in this human dream.*

These continuing connections reassure me, but I miss the touch of that great Greek who danced liked Zorba.

Epilogue

Without End

Chapter One

Ancient Mysteries

In 1995, I stood in a tomb in the Valley of the Kings staring at a picture of Isis, the Egyptian Mother God, painted on the wall in antiquity. In the next panel, Isis the goddess of life had transformed into the Lion-headed Sekhmet—the warrior goddess with sword in hand ready to avenge the murder of Osiris—the husband of Isis. These gods and goddesses embodied behaviors and emotions common to their human subjects—life and death, love and passion, grief and suffering, murder and revenge. At that time, I stiffened against the avenging goddess and leaned toward the compassionate Isis. I didn't consider myself a warrior. Yet here I was in December 2009 back in Egypt seeking an encounter with the fierce, feline goddess Sekhmet. It was she who called me here.

In 2008, I'd read about an upcoming pilgrimage to Egypt to be led by Hank Wesselman, an anthropologist who practiced shamanism. I read of his incredible encounter with this Goddess Sekhmet housed at a shrine in Karnac since 1450 BC. She actually "spoke" to him. And, in a moment of ecstasy, he embraced and kissed her. It filled me with a longing for a similar experience with this alleged "living statue"—a seven-foot black stone image of a slender human female with a lion's head crowned by a sun disc and a cobra at the center of her forehead. "Yes!" I said to myself. "I want to go to Egypt with this man. I want to embrace this goddess."

But in 2008, consideration for my husband's health kept me from leaving the country and I let go of the Egyptian fantasy. In 2009 Mitch died on the 20th day of March, the first day of spring. The land of pyramids and tombs that honored the dead beckoned.

Over 40 people of assorted ages and various stages of life from several countries around the world had gathered for the Shamanic Sojourn. We all met in Cairo on December 3, 2009—the desert home of ancient mysteries. My journey had been long and the jetlag left me weary, but the first night I woke at midnight in the famous Mena House Hotel—wide awake and unable to sleep. Fortunately, my roommate slept soundly. I made myself a cup of hot chocolate, propped myself up in bed and wrote in my journal: "**December 4**: My birthday as foretold in a recent dream; a time of new beginnings. I wonder what the day will bring? I dedicate myself to this pilgrimage. May my spirits and guardians protect me, direct my steps to where I need to be, and enlighten my mind with what I need to know."

"I just heard you were 77 years old and climbed into the Red Pyramid," a fellow sojourner exclaimed as she rushed up to me at the end of the first day. "I'm amazed."

"So?" My response sounded sharp. *Did she think me a tottering old woman? Of course I climbed into the pyramid.* And, later that night on a Nile dinner cruise, embraced by the foreign ambience, the Egyptian music emboldened my soul and in a moment of rapturous abandonment I joined the belly dancers. Hank, the group leader observed, "You must have been wild in the 60s!" I smiled to myself and thought *I still am.*

On December 5th we toured the Cairo Museum. I had been there before, but did not remember this particular larger than life-size black marble statue of Sekhmet. As I looked up into her face, the lion head gazed straight ahead with an impersonal stare. She captivated me. My breath stopped and my heart raced as I bowed to honor her and beseeched her mercy. "I came," I whispered and wondered where we'd meet again. The next day the group flew to Luxor.

Paying Attention

Strolling through the airport, I heard a repeated metal click as I walked and stopped to examine the bottom of my sandals. Shocked, I found a tiny guardian angel pin stuck to the rubber sole. Before leaving home I had attached this pin to my daypack. Somehow it had fallen off and I stepped on it with my right foot. I retrieved the unbroken pin and replaced it on my shoulder bag. *What was that all about?* I wondered. *Was it a good or bad omen? Pay attention!*

The following morning at 5:00 AM I awoke in the St. George Luxor Hotel to the haunting sounds of soulfully chanted prayers wafting through the windows. The Muslims stop five times a day wherever they are to offer their prayers, a gentle reminder to me. Pay attention and honor the divinity within and without, even on the sole of my shoe that guides my steps.

I wrote in my journal: *"**December 6**: Off to Abydos and Dendara today, to the House of Osiris, the place of resurrection. It seems that Ancient Egyptians had a preoccupation with death, believing this life to be a preparation for the next one. Pay attention!"*

The Egyptologist guided us through the Osirium, the place that honored the resurrection of King Osiris (his wife Isis had restored his life after his brother Set murdered him). Cut into the rocks, the underground chambers looked like open tombs and in previous times the Nile waters regularly flooded this sacred site submerging all the tombs. Then when the water receded, the tombs reappeared as if resurrected or restored. Of course now, the Aswan Dam controlls the Nile and only the birds fly in and out of the dry open tombs. As they soar into the light from the darkness, the winged ones create a beautiful sight and an unearthly sound.

Everywhere, I saw wings. Inside the temple, I saw wings carved in stone—the feathered wings of Isis, the Goddess who restored life to Osiris, the wings of Maat, the Goddess who represented Justice, and the wings of Horus, the Falcon God. Outside, multitudes of gray swallows flew in and out of the tombs, creating an eerie drama uniting the past with the present. "Fly away home," I urged the aerial messengers. But I knew from my recent experiences of guiding Mitch's soul after his death that spirits came and went as they chose. The birds swooped in and out of the tombs.

Later in Dendara at the Temple honoring the Goddess Hathor, I stood in line for the bathroom. When I went inside, my mother's butterfly ring that I wore caught in the hem of my blouse when I rose from the toilet. It threw me off balance. In order to stand up straight, I had to take off the ring. It fell to the floor and in the darkness, I couldn't find it. I hesitated spending more time. Fortunately, Ellen, the next woman in line, had a flashlight and we found the ring. This is the same woman who admired my bravery, in spite of my age. She seemed to have an interesting role on this journey. *Pay attention.*

"Tell me about all your rings," Suzanna, a fellow pilgrim, had asked me that morning at breakfast.

"I'd love to. Maybe later today," I responded.

"Well, each ring has a story," I began as we sat together on the bus ride from Dendara. Showing her my mother's ring I related, "It took me three years after her death in 2006 before I could wear it because of our difficult relationship, and today I almost lost it in the toilet." I hesitated. "You know what? It just occurred to me. In order to embrace the energy of Sekhmet I need to let go of my mother's energy. Forgive and move on. Tomorrow we visit Karnac and Sekhmet waits." I took off my mother's ring and put it in my purse.

"That's quite an epiphany," Suzanna remarked.

Karnac

We arrived early on December 8th at the Karnac temple, my excitement mingled with the cool desert air as we disembarked from the bus. A multitude of shrines that honor the ancient gods and goddesses compose this immense temple over 4000 years old. Constructed by thousands of builders over hundreds of years on such a monumental scale that its mystery continues to boggle the modern technological mind.

The rising sun cast shadows around the massive stone pillars in this desert sanctuary as I waited expectantly to enter the Shrine of Ptah. "The word 'Egypt' means 'The land of Ptah,'" our guide related. This deity is said to have come from the stars and formed the world by speaking it into being with his words and governed Egypt for 8000 years. Sekhmet, the great transformation lion-headed goddess, ruled at his side as his wife and sister. Other stories say that although Ptah is the "Creator God," Sekhmet pre-existed him. She is considered to be the "Primal and Supreme Creative Power." I anxiously awaited our encounter.

The group gathered to begin our tour and I noticed a frown cross Hank's face as he spoke quietly to the Egyptologist. "I'm sorry to tell you that the Shrine of Ptah is closed for restoration," Hank addressed our group. "We will not be able to visit the statue of Sekhmet and have the private audience I promised."

"But that's why I came," my voice cracked as I spoke out.

"I will go see for myself if there is anyway we can get in. I know this is a disappointment for many of you." Hank left to check out the Shrine of Ptah and the group followed the Egyptologist to explore the other parts of the immense ruins on the outside grounds. I walked slowly hardly paying attention.

When Hank caught up with the group, his obvious frustration said it all. "There is no way we can get in," he reported. "Scaffolding is everywhere and the statues are removed or covered. Yesterday they turned away a group from France that came to Egypt just to see this site. I'm sorry."

The eternal optimist in me held back the tears. *Surely something good will happen.* Then Suzanna, the friend who loved my rings and stories, spoke up. "Back down the path, Lawrence and I passed a damaged statue that looked like Sekhmet. If any of you want to see it we'll lead the way when our tour here is done." Our guide said he was finished and gave us 90 minutes to wander around on our own before we met back at the entrance. Several of us turned and quickly followed Suzanna and Lawrence—her Greek husband who reminded me of Mitch.

We found three weathered basalt statues of seated goddesses. Each had its own cubicle separating it from the others by a waist high stone wall. Each had its own entrance. The battered statue in the middle looked like Sekhmet, but time had taken its toll and it wasn't clear. I carried my book, *The Goddess Sekhmet,* by Robert Masters and had planned to read the *Invocation to Sekhmet* at her indoor shrine. Searching through the pages, I found a picture that seemed to match the statue in front of me. The left hand, outstretched on her lap held an ankh—a symbol of life. As I sought confirmation from others, I noticed Maria, another group member, had already moved inside and knelt prayerfully beside the statue. Enough talk, I wanted to be next.

When Maria left I stepped into the entrance of the small enclave and stood before the seated life-size black image of the goddess. I took off my shoes, my sunglasses and my hat then placed my shawl over my head and bowed in supplication at the feet of the statue. Looking into her face, partially worn away by centuries of time, I asked for a sign. Silence.

Hoping for something tangible from this age-weathered goddess, I only heard someone humming. Then knowing others waited, I replaced my shoes, put on my hat and my sunglasses and stepped out of the portal disappointed. Leaning against a stone wall so as not to block the path, I began reading aloud the *Invocation of Sekhmet* from my book.

"As it was at Memphis
So be it now!
Hear me, I beseech Thee,
O Powerful One!" (On and on I read, my voice rising in adoration)

"Sekhmet,
Life-Giver to the Gods,
Sekhmet,
Lady of Flame,
Sekhmet,
Great One of Magic,
Sekhmet,
Scorching Eye of Ra,
Sekhmet,
Holy is Thy Name! ..." (in petition I continued)

"Do not consume us
With thy Fire,
Give us Light! ..." (then reading on to the end)

"At the Throne of Silence,
even, shall no more
be spoken than
Encircling One!

"I lose myself in Thee!"

With tears in my eyes, I finished the Invocation oblivious to those gathered around. A force shook my body; I couldn't move. Not wanting to leave Her presence, once more I slipped off my sandals, my hat and my sunglasses then covered my head with my shawl. I leaned against the rock, my arms folded across my chest with clenched fists, thumbs upright, and eyes closed. Again I heard the humming vibration and realized it came from me.

Almost in a trance, I sensed people coming and going on the path. Then I heard someone sobbing and my eyes snapped open. Judy, a fellow pilgrim of Japanese descent, supported by her friend Lee Ann, huddled at the feet of the scarred statue crying. Judy battled fourth stage cancer, now she sought the strength of the warrior goddess. I called on my spiritual helpers to create a protective and safe space for Judy's supplication. Quietly, I started chanting, "Do not consume us with Thy Fire, give us Light; Do not consume us with Thy Fire, give us Light" over and over again.

"Don't put water on the statue!" A male voice shouted and I wondered if Judy had anointed the statue of Sekhmet. With my eyes still closed I envisioned Mary Magdalene anointing the feet of Jesus with her tears and wiping them with her hair. Then an angry male voice shouted out something in Arabic. Unable to understand, but not wanting to open my eyes and break my meditation, I assumed a tourist was misbehaving. Then I heard a melody that sounded like a cell phone. These distractions in present time temporarily disrupted my connection with ancient times, but I kept humming and chanting. Soon everything grew quiet and I lingered in no time.

Then again the sound of crying, I opened my eyes. Judy had returned. She crouched on the ground with her arms around Sekhmet and Lee Ann sat beside her. I continued to hold sacred space. As they left I surrounded them with my arms and whispered three times, "Do not consume us with Thy Fire. Give us Light."

Once more, with closed eyes and bowed head, I took up my place outside the gateway to the goddess. Time passed. When I looked again the shrine stood empty, everyone had moved on. Once more I entered the holy enclosure and knelt in front of Sekhmet, "The Primal and Supreme Creative Power." Placing my right hand on her left hand that held the ankh, I asked for the blessing of Life. In my mind, I heard the ancient rocks cry out her name, and I picked up a pebble from this place in remembrance.

Retreating from her presence, I replaced my sandals, my hat and my sunglasses then turned to walk down the path. A slim Egyptian man dressed in a suit stood a few feet away quietly watching. He bowed to me with his hands folded in prayer as I walked by. I bowed in return.

After my encounter with the goddess, I felt disoriented and looked around to find my direction and then moved slowly toward the entrance, still not quite sure what had happened. Suzanna caught up with me and shared this story.

"As Lawrence and I watched while you stood chanting outside Sekhmet's enclosure, one of the guards came over and started cursing. 'What kind of person would do something like that?' Then he called to the other guards; they were ready to escort you out (that was the Arabic shouting I heard). Lawrence bribed them and they all left. A plainclothes tourist policeman, assigned to our group, then came over and stood by quietly."

"I saw him as I left," I said. "He bowed to me."

"It was quite an amazing experience," Suzanna continued. "I saw a dazzling light surrounding you. You looked like a priestess, but some people walked by and didn't seem to notice, almost as if you were invisible."

"Thank you Suzanna and thank that Greek husband of yours for being my guardian angels. I had no idea what was going on, but I love that the masculine and feminine energies worked together. It feels like a connection with Mitch."

Walking to a bench at the entrance to wait for the group, I sat down and began jotting my thoughts in my journal. "Wow! What an experience. That never could have happened in the indoor temple of Sekhmet for the promised two or three minutes. I wonder why the guard was so angry at my behavior and yelled at me or was he upset at the women putting water on the statue?" It suddenly dawned on me that this may not be the only time I'm misunderstood. *Don't be surprised if others misinterpret your behavior and your writing and then criticize you*, I said to myself.

Temple of Isis at Philae

December 10: Our group boarded a motor boat to visit the temple on the island of Philae dedicated to Isis. Originally worshippers built this temple and shrine on another island near by, but the Aswan dam redirected the Nile and submerged that island under water. Workmen transported every artifact, piece by piece, stone by stone, to Philae and resurrected the temple so this ancient pilgrimage would not be lost.

On my last trip in 1995, I visited Philae with a group and then the next day returned by myself to spend several hours at the shrine. By evening all the other visitors had left and I was the lone tourist on the island until later when a man and his wife showed up for the Light Show and then there were three of us. So this time with hundreds of clamoring tourists crowding inside the ruins, I decided to spend most of my time outside. Lingering by the water, I saw in my mind's eye the transition of the sacred stones to this island. Supposedly stones hold the history of the world, I could only imagine what stories these stones had to tell.

I thought of the Temple of Isis saved from the flooding waters—her shrine snatched from the arms of destruction. I imagined Isis restoring life to the murdered Osiris—snatching her husband from the arms of death. I then envisioned Isis transforming into Sekhmet to avenge his murder. Isis, the Black Madonna, the Sacred Feminine who has inspired women for thousands of years continues to receive homage. "Oh Great Mother," I implored, "I call on you in your many manifestations: reveal to me your wisdom."

After standing on the shoreline and looking out to sea, I turned to walk up the hill and noticed several uniformed Egyptian tourist policemen scattered about the compound. One husky policeman moved in my direction and smiled as he approached. Walking up to me, he folded his hands in prayer and bowed. "Isis," he said softly.

Surprised, I searched his brown eyes and then bowed in return. "Isis," I repeated.

Then he surrounded my folded hands with his dark hands, bowed his head and whispered, "I love Isis."

With closed eyes, I bowed my head and said, "I love Isis." We both repeated the words several times in prayer. A warm, vibrating energy passed between our hands. We stood for a few minutes in the ruins of a stone archway leading to the temple from the sea. A young Egyptian policeman and an senior American tourist honored the ancient life-giving Goddess who promised Osiris and all humankind, "You shall live again forever." Then I opened my eyes and acknowledged the policeman. We bowed again to each other and I slowly walked away.

Following the path up the hill to join the others, I stopped and sat on a low stone wall to absorb the moment. In this Muslim culture men and women do not touch each other in public. This encounter boggled my mind. I could only shake my head and repeat, "I love Isis."

Abu Simbel

December 11: Over 3000 years ago two massive rock temples were carved into a mountain in Southern Egypt. In the 1960s, when the Aswan Dam redirected the Nile and threatened their destruction, UNESCO oversaw their removal and reconstruction at the present site. I stood transfixed by the magnificent temple featuring four gigantic statues of Ramesses II and the other temple of his wife Nefertari, dedicated to Hathor. The pharaoh and his wife appear as gods dwarfing us humans entering their sanctuary. Stepping into the temple of Ramesses II from the bright sunlight, I paused for a moment and then turned to look at the huge images painted on the wall. Sekhmet greeted me. She stood behind Ramesses II with her hands on his shoulders giving him the strength he needed to smite his enemies. Other Egyptian kings called on this warrior goddess following the lead of the Sun God Ra who, when in desperation of losing his kingdom, summoned her might to help win his war. I wondered how often throughout history Sekhmet's powers had been invoked and how often they had been abused.

Circling through the immense pillars and stretching my neck to view the impressive frescos, I saw Sekhmet honored many times. Then I found my way to a rather small empty chamber in the back corner of the temple where once more the walls revealed Sekhmet blessing the king. I quietly entered to pay my respects and spent a few moments in meditation. As I turned to leave I saw Judy's husband standing alone waiting and then recognized Judy kneeling in prayer in front of another image of Sekhmet. I stopped and stood in silence to hold the power that permeated the room. Judy didn't look surprised when she finished her prayers, rose up, and saw me. We bowed again to each other and acknowledged the spirit at work.

The Great Pyramid

December 12: The last day before departing for home we traveled to the Great Pyramid and Giza Plateau. Most of the group rode camels. I chose to walk and wandered alone around the sacred grounds climbing over crumbling rocks and ruins laid by unknown hands so many centuries before. Seeking to absorb the energy and memories that lingered, I touched the ancient stones and asked for their wisdom. When a hawk flew overhead, I acknowledged the majesty of Horus, the Sun God, still watching.

I strolled among the many tombs, so many tombs, so honoring of life after death. *What secrets do you hold?* I wondered to myself. *The ancient Egyptians used this life to prepare for the next one and did not fear death. What can we learn from that civilization to help us today?* I continued my search through those age-old ruins seeking an answer to the mystery.

Later that evening, after tourist hours, our guides had arranged for our group to enter the King's Chamber of the Great Pyramid and remain there for 90 minutes. In single file we each hunched over to climb through the narrow and dark passage of seemingly endless stairs leading up to the King's Chamber. Hank carried his drum. After crouching through the entryway, my eyes adjusted to the dimly lit room and I crossed over and sat down leaning against the empty stone sarcophagus. "This is a rare opportunity," Hank explained to the group "I will drum while you journey. Try to connect with ancient deities or the spirits of this sacred place, some believe this pyramid to be a 'Stargate,' a portal for Light Beings." Hank picked up the drum reverently and began the steady beat that echoed throughout the King's Chamber.

Weary in mind and body from my morning's spiritual quest, I decided to just sit and hold sacred space in hopes that the Stargate would open and the Light Beings would find me. I wove in and out of consciousness. After the last sound of the drumbeat, we all sat in silence. Time passed. Several group members reported their visions, but my day had been fulfilled. I felt tired and ready to go home.

Chapter Two

Recognition

After returning home, I realized that fate had intervened and set the stage for me to meet the age-weathered and battered image of the goddess whom I had trouble recognizing. It reminded me of an incident a few years previous when a visiting neighbor stood in front of a portrait painted of me at about age forty and asked, "Who is that beautiful woman?" *Good god lady*, I thought. *Can't you see it's me?*

At Karnac, when I stood in front of the black seated statue of the lion-headed warrior goddess, whose ears and face were partially eaten away by time, missing the sun disk and cobra that identifies her power, I asked: "Is this Sekhmet?" Then, when I saw the ankh she carried, the symbol of life and power, and felt her immortal spirit in that broken image, I *knew*.

Thinking about my relationship with that ancient goddess, I jotted some notes in my journal. "The comments from fellow sojourners about my age still ring in my ears: *I heard you were 77 years old and climbed into the Red Pyramid, I'm amazed. You must have been something in the 60's. It's so great that you 'hang in.'* Those people looked at me and only saw this old body. I wanted to scream at them: *Can't you see me?*"

Is young the opposite of old? I pondered and continued writing. "I will never be young again. The broken image of Sekhmet will never be whole again. We are caricatures of our former selves in the continuing transmutation called life, but the power is not diminished. Sekhmet's power is real: Isis called on her to avenge the death of her husband Osiris. The kings and pharaohs called on her strength to smite their enemies. No matter her physical appearance, no matter how aged and weathered, no matter how battered the basalt form—I know the spirit, the power, the might stands ready and able. She is a force to be reckoned with. And, this is the goddess who called to me in my old age. She is the goddess who destroys the old for the new to be born. I now believe that *new* is the opposite of old."

My pen stopped in midair, a thought crossed my mind. *Didn't I have a vivid dream years ago about an "Old Woman?"* Remembering the poem I wrote, I searched through my files and finally found it—written in 1986.

Dream

Her prune shriveled body
next to mine
Repulsion
My mouth drawn to her
cracked thin lips
Connection
Eyes closed, passion stirs,
sensual warmth
Surprise
Old woman, it is You,
it is me.
Recognition
Woman, it is time,
honor thy self
Celebration.

She—the Old Woman whose "prune-shriveled" body laid next to mine in that dream 24 years ago. She—the Old Woman whose cracked thin lips drew me for a kiss and warmed me with her sensual pleasure. She—the Old Woman I recognized as me. She is the Ancient Goddess.

Meditating on this I realized it was the following year—1987, when I first heard the story of Sekhmet at a Jungian book fair in Claremont California. At that time, I didn't know what to do with that warrior image, that fierce goddess frightened me.

In 1985, Mitch and I had married. That handsome Great Greek loved me dearly. He recognized in me the powerful, fierce feminine, but was never threatened. On occasion when I yelled at him with a dark fury that surprised even me, he only nodded and respected the need for my outrage. He *knew* me before I knew myself and supported my inner and outer journeys. Now, after his death, I continue to feel his support helping this old lion-hearted goddess recognize herself.

When I rummaged through my files that night looking for the poem, I also found an eight-page love letter Mitch wrote to me on April 19, 1985—a few months before we married. His letter begins with mention of our special connections and it ends with:

> *I also believe that the number of connections, yet to be "awakened" and made are infinite—like Space and we will never complete the process during our lifetime. Karmic energy will continue into the next zone. The Love Affaire goes on—eternally.*

The poem, the letter and the ideas from almost a quarter of a century ago connect me to the Now—this moment. My spirit waited for my body to catch up—to age to perfection. No wonder I enjoy a good wine.

Reflecting back on my three Egyptian sojourns, I realize that this ancient land of pyramids and tombs vibrates with an energy that words cannot describe nor thoughts discern. It penetrates the soul and can be perceived in the body instinctively through the senses. I first visited this place that honors the continuity of life and death and life again soon after Mitch and I married and returned soon after his death.

Not long ago, as I lay in bed in the early morning, my mind wrestled with the meaning of the past 25 years and what comes next. In the darkness, I heard an inner voice: *In 1986, I appeared in your dream as the Old Woman. In 1987, I called you to Egypt for the first time to honor me in the form of Isis. In 1995, you returned and saw me, transformed into a lion-headed warrior, painted on the wall of a tomb ready to avenge the murder of Osiris. I frightened you. You weren't ready. You needed more time.*

In 2009, I called you to Egypt again. You came. That's when the others recognized you as the Old Woman. Yes, you can climb pyramids. Yes, you can keep up. Yes, you can dance. But, you are the Old Woman. Most people ignore old women as irrelevant—a reminder of their own mortality. This is changing. Sekhmet is the goddess of transformation. You have been anointed and carry her power. Who fears an old female lion? You may be surprised. Mitch loved that powerful fierce feminine in you and you helped him to wake up. Now it is your turn. He is helping you from the otherside. WAKE UP NOW! Recognize who you are.

"YES!" I pulled out my journal and wrote furiously, "YES! I struggle with a leaky bladder. YES! I pause when I stand to brace my arthritic knee and always bring up the rear on a hike. YES! My vision blurs in the nightlight—I struggle to read the print in the phone book—I forget where I put my glasses. YES! The physical body ages, but the spirit is ageless. My grandson recognized that recently when discussing aging relatives, he said to me: 'J.J., you don't count, you have goddess power.' That power comes from the Ancient One—the Great Goddess—Wisdom. Bestowed in Her own time and in Her own way."

"YES!" I can now say to the world: "Look at me! Don't turn your eyes away. Don't ignore the Old Woman who stands before you, who comes in your dreams, who waits for you."

Chapter Three

Nessa's Journey

Prior to my journey to Egypt in December 2009, I had distributed samples of my memoir—*Spiritual Midwife* to interested parties. An executive editor of a San Francisco book house liked my story telling well enough to consider the book for publication. She requested the completed manuscript and promised a decision after the holidays. Returning home from my trip, I anxiously awaited her reply.

Over the New Year's weekend, Deena, my daughter-in-law, told me that her mother, a long time victim of Alzheimer's Disease, had taken neither food nor drink in almost two weeks. She was non-responsive. She was dying. She almost died a few months before, but then revived. Death is sometimes a difficult appointment to keep.

"Would you like me to go and play my harp for her?" I offered. "I can perform a cleansing ritual of the chakra points that often hold negative energy like anger. It might help her to let go."

"Oh would you do that?" Deena asked. "I'd really appreciate it. My mother probably is very angry. She didn't plan to die like this!"

On Wednesday afternoon, January 6th with my small harp in hand, I visited Nessa in her darkened room at the care facility. She lay in bed and seemed asleep. "It's Jacqueline," I whispered. No response. "May I play the harp for you and offer a ritual?" She swallowed. After unpacking my harp I pulled up a chair and started strumming the strings that filled the air with harmonious vibrations. A light flickered in the room; I accepted that as a sign to continue.

After clearing my own self of negative emotions, I then turned to Nessa. Calling in the light and sounding the chords on the harp, I visualized the light moving from the soles of her feet to the crown of her head dissolving the anger, greed, ignorance, doubt, jealousy and pride, then I pictured radiant beams of love filling her body. *May the Mother Light shine upon you. May all love and compassion surround you and may the Child Light within you, guide you safely home,* I prayed. At that moment Nessa's eyes blinked open and shut. I believed she accepted the blessing.

The next day Deena said her mother seemed more at peace that night when she visited. I offered to go again. She agreed. "I'll go every day 'til she passes," I promised, thinking it would be two or three days.

That night Nessa came to me in a dream. She told me it was hard to keep the old traditions. Nessa is Jewish so I wondered about any special rites around death and dying in her religion. Her daughter did not actively practice the Jewish faith, but found information on the Internet. The next day she brought prayers to read for her mother and invited Marlis to help—a woman from the Jewish community who worked with the dying. We all watched Nessa as she paused for long stretches between breaths thinking each one to be her last. She lingered on.

January 10, another dream came. Nessa appeared dead. I heard her name being called, but also another name I didn't recognize. A sheet of unfamiliar letters floated over her body and I assumed they were Hebrew. This was now the sixth day and each day I had played and performed the cleansing ritual. "Maybe we need a Rabbi," I suggested to Deena. On the seventh day she brought a CD with a Rabbi chanting and singing in Hebrew and left it playing softly. Her mother continued to linger.

On day eight I arrived in the early afternoon. Nessa's breathing had changed to fast and shallow. Greeting her, I again asked for permission to play. No response. I knew some of Nessa's family had died in the holocaust and forgiveness might be an issue. *Could that hold her back?* I wondered. Feeling frustrated at what to do next, I invoked the wisdom of the grandmothers who I believe stand by ready to serve. Certainly they would know what to do. I looked up and saw a picture of Nessa's grandmother hanging on the wall by her bed.

Marlis knocked then entered the darkened room bringing another woman from the Jewish community with her. They came armed with books and Psalms to read. Deena arrived and they lovingly read and sang Holy Words to Nessa in Hebrew as well as English—"The Lord is my Shepherd, I shall not want… ." A Rabbi gently chanted prayers on the CD in the background. I sat holding sacred space with the spirit of the grandmothers. Marlis' friend offered Deena her Star of David necklace and she placed it gently around her mother's neck. I had another appointment and left at dusk. The others went shortly thereafter leaving Nessa surrounded with loving energy and the soft chanting on the CD. She passed quietly the following morning at 3:00 A.M.

Several days later in a dream I saw Nessa at the airport. I had come to see her off. She guided several children in front of her as she passed through the gates. Eventually they found their way to the plane. I witnessed their ascension.

My time with Nessa became a gift while I waited news of my memoir. The book speaks of my many journeys, some assisting people to die well, but mostly guiding departed souls needing help to move on to the light. It ends with the story of my husband before and after his death. *Maybe, just maybe, the book is incomplete,* I thought. My experience with Nessa indicates that with help we can do the work and let go of negative attachments *before* we die. Then we are free to fly home non-stop. I did not help Nessa to die, but to wake up and ascend.

Chapter Four

Spirit At Work

With the fate of my book still hanging, I wanted to explore further the idea of "waking up before you die." I trusted that spirit would provide the opportunities and guide my steps.

January 21, 2010: "I brought the book before my editorial board today and the publisher just didn't think we would publish this book well," the e-mail informed me. Signed with regrets from the Executive Editor who had believed in my book and still encouraged me not to give up.

The disappointment stung, but the eternal optimist in me looked for the silver lining. Much like my reaction in Egypt when I learned about the closure of Sekhmet's Shrine—*there must a reason—something more awaits my discovery.*

On a return e-mail to the editor, I thanked her and acknowledged that the rejection had helped confirm my gut feeling that the full story had yet to be told. A short three weeks later a surprise phone call from a hospice social worker revealed the next step on my journey.

"Are you still guardian for Cindy?" the social worker inquired. "The doctor has referred her to hospice because she has stopped eating and drinking and refuses all medications."

A few years earlier I had assisted Cindy, a mid-age physically disabled client. She had suffered severe nerve and brain damage as a teenager after attempting suicide with carbon monoxide over a failed love affair. Confined to a wheel chair all these years, she could barely feed herself and had trouble communicating, but her mind seemed clear. She loved music and thrived on attention. Until her death a few years before, Cindy's mother tended to her needs. After the loss of her mother, Cindy seemed to blossom in an assisted living facility where the staff gave her lots of support. Her estranged sister lived in New York and visited infrequently. I had volunteered to do Cindy's accounting and shared lunch and special occasions with her. That was two years ago, now this call from hospice.

"I know it's none of my business, but what happened?" I asked

"Apparently she had feelings for someone at the facility and found they weren't reciprocated. She got depressed and refused to eat, she wouldn't even let the staff clean her colostomy bag. I found your name in her papers and we need someone responsible to sign for her."

"Well, I'm sorry to hear this, but I no longer work with Cindy, " I replied. "Do you know she has a sister in New York?"

"Yes, but Cindy doesn't want her involved. I'll keep looking for someone else to help. Thank you."

After hanging up with the social worker, I called Cindy's assisted living facility and asked for the administrator whom I knew. I inquired about what had happened.

"Cindy had an unfortunate incident here," she related, "and is very angry. She's at Hospice House now, but I must warn you, she's upset and doesn't want visitors."

"Maybe I can take my harp and play for her or do some kind of ritual," I suggested.

"Go quickly," she confided. "Cindy hasn't eaten or taken liquids for two weeks and may not last much longer."

I hate to see Cindy die angry or depressed, I thought to myself. *The least I can do is help her die peacefully.* Remembering that Nessa, although unresponsive, finally let go and moved on with some help, I hoped Cindy would accept help as well. I drove to Hospice House that afternoon.

The nurse directed me to Cindy's darkened room. Several stuffed animals sat around on the couch and a vase of spring flowers added color. Cindy slept. Not wanting to disturb her, thinking she might ask me to leave, I quietly pulled up a chair by the bed and observed her deep breathing. Her ordeal had taken its toll; her gaunt face looked aged beyond her 55 years.

"Cindy, it is Jacqueline. Would you mind if a said a little prayer for you?" Her dark eyes opened and she looked at me, but did not respond, then her eyes closed. Since she didn't refuse or order me out, I considered it an affirmative. Then visualizing light surrounding her bedside, I cleared my own energy field first.

Since I hadn't brought my harp, I performed the ritual without the harmonic chords. Calling in her spiritual helpers and guardian angels, I asked for their guidance and support and let the surrounding light bathe her body. Her face relaxed. I began the ritual of cleansing the negative emotions at the soles of her feet where anger often accumulates and visualized the anger dissolve into the light. Then my concentration moved up to the base of her spine and to the other energy centers, dissolving greed, ignorance, doubt, jealousy and pride and any other emotions that might keep her from a good transition. I continued to bathe her in the Holy and Transforming Light as she slept peacefully. *May the Mother Light shine upon you*, I offered my prayer for her well being. *May all love and compassion surround you*, I continued. *May the Child Light within you, guide you safely home.* Sitting awhile longer, I lingered in silence, then calmly left the room.

"She's sleeping," I told the clerk at the desk. "I'll be back tomorrow."

Returning the next day to do another cleansing, I found the room brighter, Cindy had just had her bath and looked refreshed. When I started to shut the door she shook her head indicating "no." I sat down by her bedside. She didn't seem to recognize me and closed her eyes. Softly I asked, "Might I do a cleansing prayer for you?" Cindy did not object. Again, I surrounded her in light and repeated the ritual. As I got ready to leave, she said, "I'm thirsty."

At the nurse's station, I reported her request. "But she hasn't been eating or drinking at all," the clerk looked perplexed. "I'll tell the nurse and she can wet her lips with some water and rinse out her mouth." I thanked her and left.

The next day the hospice nurse called me and said that morning Cindy had asked for something to drink then consumed three cups of tea. "We were shocked," she went on. "We totally support her decision, but she can't stay here any longer since she's obviously changed her mind about dying. We'll have to move her to a foster care home."

Oh my god! I thought to myself. *The ritual must have helped Cindy let go of her anger and depression and now she wants to live. I didn't expect that, but one never knows how spirit works!*

I did know the owner of the foster care home who took Cindy under her wing. She surrounds her residents with care, good food, love and attention. Cindy is in good hands. It appears some people can wake up in this life before they die and some can't, but hope never dies.

About this same time, I awoke from a dream filled with gratitude. Ron, my ex-husband, had died alone six years before in an alcoholic stupor. I had not seen him in over 25 years. After his death, whenever Ron entered my dreams he'd be searching for me and I always tried to avoid him. Over time, in hopes of helping, I had played the harp and performed many rituals for him, but never received any indication of their success; he still pursued me. But in this dream we appeared together having just finished a two-year graduate program for senior counselors. Some of the other graduates grumbled at the additional work and more difficult cases, but Ron made no complaints. Poised, in a pale blue monastic robe, he appeared at peace with himself. Ron bowed to me, then kissed me lightly and gave me a warm embrace. Proud of his accomplishment, he went off to do his work.

While alive, Ron had been a spiritual being trapped in a body addicted to alcohol. He had lost the battle, but obviously not the war. Although he "haunted" me for many years in my dreams, he now had graduated—a reason to never lose hope. It is never too late to heal.

Mitch had expressed a desire to become a more spiritual being before his death, then three months after he died, he appeared in my dream looking robust and said: "I just woke up." In my dream about Ron, it took him six years to "graduate." I dreamt Nessa ascended shortly after her death and Cindy woke up before she died. I'm amazed at what my dreams are revealing, what can happen to people in transition from this life to the next. Death is not an end, but a beginning and provides a setting for the soul to "wake up" or "graduate." Spirit at work!

Chapter Five

Stargate

In March 2010, I sat with a small group in a circle on the third day of a Shamanic Vision Seeker workshop at the Breitenbush Retreat Center in the Oregon Cascades. At this gathering, we had established contact with the world of spirit helpers, teachers and ancestors—the world of no time, soul time, and dreamtime.

Our leader, Hank Wesselman, explained that our interest in shamanism probably meant we had an ancestor who had similar interests as a shaman, a mystic, a medicine person or a healer—the "gift" seems to run in families. On our next shamanic journey, we would look for that ancestor to become our spirit helper. I knew my Tennessee Grandma Mary Jo had special gifts and helped her neighboring farm folk pass when it came their time to die—a spiritual midwife. But I hoped to find someone else further back, maybe an indigenous shaman, or a Celtic Druid like Merlin with a long beard and a fancy robe, someone more magical, more glamorous than a hillbilly farmer. So I felt disappointed when on my shamanic journey, I found Grandma Mary Jo waiting for me in a faded housedress wiping her hands on a dirty white apron.

Grandma just stood there and laughed. "Sakes alive child, I don't know nothin' 'bout any of them fancy dresses or strange people. I just feed the chickens and carry water and do my chores. When a neighbor's close to dyin' they come and fetch me to help. I see a light go out over the dyin' and help 'em cross over. But in the mornin' I still get up to bake the biscuits and feed the chickens, a body's got to have somethin' to fuss at." She shook her head.

Then I laughed. Maybe it disturbed the group, but I couldn't help it. My laughing rang out and I heard Hank comment, "Someone got it." I laughed at my self; I laughed at my highfalutin ideas. I laughed until I cried. "Oh Grandma, I love you!" I hugged her. "We are family."

The laughter was healing. The laughter punctured the big balloon of my inflated ego and dumped me back to earth with a thud. It wasn't what I intended. The jolt shattered my illusions and woke me up; it helped me understand where I came from and possibly where I'm going—an unexpected gift from the spirits.

The decision to attend the workshop began with a dream six weeks before. Hank Wesselman, the anthropologist who had previously guided my Egyptian pilgrimage in December 2009, had personally invited me to attend a five-day Vision Seeker workshop at a retreat center nearby. Hank would lead the group on shamanic journeys to spirit helpers who could assist with personal guidance and healing.

From 1985 to 1996, I studied shamanism and it provided me with many moving experiences. But when my drum cracked, my rattle broke, and my sage burnt a hole in the rug, it seemed like an omen. My spiritual practice shifted to playing the harp and dream work. So I debated with myself about whether to attend another shamanic workshop; I asked for a dream to guide me. In this particular dream Hank and I stood in a boat on a river following another boat with a woman performing a ceremony and calling forth people from their tombs and graves along the riverbanks. Hank and I had the job to carve messages on the stones in six weeks. Checking the calendar, I discovered the workshop took place in just six weeks. Obviously, Hank and I had a continuing agenda. I signed up.

It snowed on the spring day at the end of March when I arrived at Brietenbush and settled in my cabin wondering who else might show up—in flesh or in spirit. That first night, 14 of us gathered in circle, men and women of assorted ages and varying shamanic experiences. I appeared to be the elder. Hank told stories and began teaching the group about shamanic journeys and how to travel outside this "reality" to otherworlds accompanied by the beat of the drum. He suggested we find our own special spiritual garden on our first journey. After stretching out, I closed my eyes and found myself in the King's Chamber at the Great Pyramid in Egypt. My mind wasn't "following directions." The old way no longer served me.

Next we journeyed to the lowerworld. "I can do this!" I said and made myself travel to the place of power animals and spirit helpers. When I arrived, a big gorilla picked me up and we swung through the forest like King Kong carrying Fay Wray. He put me in an elevator and zipped me back up to the King's Chamber in the Pyramid. I could only laugh to myself.

"This just isn't working," I told Hank the next day before the lunch break. "I will sit and hold sacred space while the others journey."

"We are going to journey for each other in partners this afternoon. There are an even number in the circle so we need you," he responded.

"Well, I'm not sure I can do justice to a partner if I can't journey to the right place for myself, but I'll think about it." Feeling frustrated, I meandered to lunch.

Barbara, a mid-age successful career woman taking her first shamanic workshop, approached me in the cafeteria line. "Would you be willing to help me? I'm having difficulty with the journeys. It's hard for me to get out of my head and you seem to have lots of experience."

"I'm willing to try and help," I offered. "I'll be your partner this afternoon, but no guarantees. Let's eat together and get better acquainted."

So when Hank instructed us to journey to the lowerworld to find a spirit helper for our partners, I decided to go directly to the King's Chamber in the Pyramid and imagine a stargate where the spirits would come to me.

As I lay next to Barbara and closed my eyes, the drumbeat took me directly to the Pyramid and a flood of rabbits came rushing through the stargate. *No, not rabbits! They're not the right kind of spirit helpers!* I tried to shoo them back. I didn't want to bring in a bunch of bunnies, but they seemed adamant: "We're prolific and we'll always be enough for her."

Then a big Warrior Rabbit jumped out in front of the pack and standing erect, he flashed his sword and shield. *Well, I hope Barbara has a sense of humor. Maybe she needs a good laugh.* I thought to myself.

Later Barbara shared with me that she had a special affinity for rabbits and her high school mascot had been a jackrabbit, she even dressed like one for a party and yes indeed, she did need to lighten up. The rabbits filled the bill.

When Barbara took her journey for me, a golden snake came slithering down a vine by a waterfall in her garden. After she told me, my first thought was *transformation*, but Hank said I must have been an Initiate in Ancient Egypt. The Initiates wore the golden snake as a band around the forehead—one is wrapped around the head mask of King Tut. *Aha! It makes sense why my journeys call me back to the Egyptian Pyramid.* I had my own path to follow.

The fourth day Hank suggested that we journey to ask for an additional spirit helper, an ancestor who loved us. I thought one of my grandmothers would emerge from the stargate, but instead my Spanish grandfather—Ubaldo Isadore, known as U.I.—showed up. *Go back, I don't want you!* I thought. He had always been so distant, so cold and unloving, it had to be a mistake. But no, my grandfather came over and put his arms around me and thanked me for helping his wife, Rosella. My grandmother had died in childbirth in 1912. In 1999, her departed spirit came to me in a dream appearing to be trapped and I helped her cross over to the Light.

"It was so hard, I didn't know what to do, how to grieve, after my Rosella died," grandfather said sadly. "My wife's death left me with six children under the age of eight. It devastated me, but I couldn't express it. I never could express my feelings and didn't know how to love my children, we gave the baby to a relative. It was the best I could do. After years of struggle the family moved to Los Angeles from New Mexico to try and make a better life far from the environment that had been so repressive."

I sat stunned. I hardly knew this man. For years my patriarchal Spanish heritage had troubled me and only recently could I acknowledge my ancestor's bravery and courage. Suddenly it dawned on me—*as my*

ancestor his blood runs through my veins and now he's here to help me.
"I am so deeply sorry, Grandpa." I touched him gently. "It must have been hard for you. I wish we'd have known each other better. After all I am your first grandchild and my daughter is your first great-grandchild. Truly, we are family."

And, it was on this same day that my Grandma Mary Jo also came to help me. I honored all my relations!

The last day, before returning home, Hank led us on one more journey to find an ancestor who needed healing. Once again I traveled to the King's Chamber in the Pyramid. My Spanish Grandfather U.I and my Hillbilly Grandma Mary Jo sat at a table drinking strong farm coffee. Grandmother Rosella came and joined them. Mary Jo suggested we go to Tennessee to heal her husband George, my redheaded grandpa. He had died of skin cancer over 60 years ago, but couldn't let go of his attachments to this life and his spirit still lingered on the farm.

We all went together. Mary Jo found George and introduced me, "This is Bert's daughter and she's come to help." He acknowledged me. I surrounded him with a healing light, a different kind of light than the damaging rays that gave him the skin cancer. My grandpa accepted the healing ritual that helped him dissolve his negative feelings. He looked transformed when we finished. Although he had never been demonstrative, George told Mary Jo that he loved her and they lay down together on the old feather bed. U.I. and Rosella left and I went back to the Pyramid for a cup of coffee. Sitting with a mug in my hand I smiled at the thought of my four grandparents together—my Council of Spiritual Elders—ready to help with whatever came next.

After returning home, I jotted some notes in my journal and recalled Hank's story of his visit to a village in Africa as an anthropologist. The tribe called their elders "The Stones." In the Native American tradition the Stone People hold the records for the Earth Mother and can be great teachers. I remembered the dream about Hank and I carving messages on stones that prodded me to attend the workshop. Then it hit me. *Oh my god!* I gasped—*I am the Village Elder—the Stone. I carry the message.*

Chapter Six

Life Demands It!

I stand at the solitary tomb on a hilltop in Crete to pay my respects. A simple cross shaped from two branches casts a shadow on the jagged and crude black marble that bears no name, no date of birth or death, only an inscription written in Greek that translates—"I hope for nothing. I fear nothing. I am free."

"Give me your blessing," I appeal to the spirit of Nikos Kazantzakis, the passionate author of *Zorba the Greek.* The exuberant esprit of Zorba, his capacity to live life to the fullest and to dance in the face of catastrophe and death has inspired *my* life for years: "Help me as I struggle to write about life and death. It has been a long journey and I have no answers."

The Greek Orthodox Church excommunicated Kazantzakis and denied his body burial in the church cemetery because of his book, *The Last Temptation of Christ.* The controversial author, who lay alone in that small park on the hilltop, portrayed Jesus as all too human as he wrestled with flesh and spirit—with life and death. Kazantzakis spoke from his own experience: "Since my youth onward, my principle anguish and source of all my joys and sorrow has been the incessant merciless battle between the spirit and the flesh…and my soul is the arena where these two armies have clashed and met."

In his spiritual autobiography—*Report to Greco,* Kazantzakis asserts there are three souls, three prayers, three stages of spiritual growth. His words speak directly to my own soul.

The first prayer: *"I am a bow in your hand, O Lord. Bend me lest I rot."*

This was my prayer after my fall from grace—my descent from the penthouse to the jailhouse on my 41st birthday. I was in danger of what Kazantzakis called "rot." From there my spiritual journey led to a more fulfilling life, something more than pleasing the body, developing the mind and seeking success. My bow definitely needed bending.

The second prayer: *"Do not bend me too much, lest I break."*

This prayer lingered on my lips about the time I first met Sekhmet, the lion-headed goddess. The thought of a bloodthirsty goddess tore at my soul. I rebelled against her call fearing a consuming rage that could destroy me or possibly others. A part of me still clung to convention.

The third prayer: *"Lord, bend me and who cares if I break."*

This prayer IS the destruction, a call to surrender. It does not bring peace of mind. It is not for a gentle soul or a gentle god or goddess. It is the cry of Sekhmet before battle. With this prayer in my heart, I cannot rest. It stirs me. It prepares me to fight or go flabby and weak. And what, at my age, is left to fight? Dylan Thomas implores—"Do not go gentle into that good night, Old age should burn and rave at close of day; Rage, rage against the dying of the light."

Growing old is not a choice, but one does not have to go flabby and weak. I embrace my flesh as well as my spirit. I love my body and do not want it to perish, nor my soul to decay. The angels and demons that once wrestled in me for control continue their war dance, but the fight is no longer between good and evil, spirit and flesh, but between order and chaos—time is the battlefield.

After writing about my experiences of guiding departed souls, that promise we wake up after death, I sought to find a way to wake up before I die. I wanted to lose all fear and welcome death, so as to "go gentle into that good night." When Sekhmet woke up after the intoxication of sleep, she had lost her rage. So I asked myself: *How do I wake up now?*

On my pilgrimage to Egypt, the age-weathered warrior goddess who met me there became my mentor. Then, on a vision quest at a retreat center, my ancestors appeared as my spiritual helpers. My Spanish ancestors traveled from Spain to Mexico City and on to a new world with the conquistadors. My Scots-Irish Celtic ancestors traveled from the borders of Ireland to the Appalachian Mountains, their restless spirits never at peace. That ancestral blood courses through my veins and blood often overrides the mind.

Yes, your friends and loved ones wait on the otherside, my blood cries out. *Yes, the afterlife is as promised—you've witnessed it, but do not cross over without a fight. You don't fight against death; you fight to live fully. Life demands it! Without death we could not be courageous. Rage, rage against the injustice of a life cut too short, of a life lived in bondage or a life lived without passion.*

I accept the challenge. The "Old Woman" in me looks into the mirror and declares: "I ain't dead yet!" She girds her loins to fight one more battle, write one more book, and take one last adventure. And ten years from now, when she looks into the mirror again, this old lion will probably roar back her head and proclaim: "Tomorrow is a good day to die. But today, I have one more battle, one more book and one more adventure. And meantime, I will live in my soul and dance!"

BIBLIOGRAPHY

Andrews, Ted. *Sacred Sounds.* St Paul: Llewellyn Publications, 1998

Andronicos, Manelis. *Delphi.* Athens: Ekdotike Athenon S.A., 1985

Baigent, Michael; Leigh, Richard; Lincoln, Henry. *Holy Blood, Holy Grail.* New York: Dell Publishing, 1982

Begg, Ean. *The Cult of the Black Virgin.* Boston: Arkana, 1985

Blair, Lawrence. *Rhythms of Vision.* New York: Schocken, 1976

Botkin, Allaln. *Induced After Death Communication: A New Therapy for Healing Grief and Trauma.* Hampton Roads, 2005

Brown, Dan. *The Da Vinci Code,* New York: Double Day, 2003

Budge, Wallis. *The Egyptian Book of the Dead.* University Books, 1960

Capra, Fritjof. *Tao of Physics.* Cambridge University Press, 1975

Didion, Joan. *The Year of Magical Thinking.* New York, Vintage Books, 2007

Downing, Christine. *The Goddess: Mythological Images of the Feminine.* New York: Crossroad, 1984

Dunnington, Jacqueline Orsini. *Guadalupe: Our Lady of New Mexico.* Santa Fe: Museum of New Mexico Press, 1999

Estes, Clarissa Pinkola, *Women Who Run With The Wolves.* New York: Ballantine Books, 1992

Fields, Virginia; Zamudio-Taylor, Victor. *The Road to Aztlan: Art From a Mythic Homeland* Los Angeles Museum of Art, 2001.

Guggenheim, Bill and Judy. *Hello From Heaven.* Bantam Books, 1997

Halifax, Joan. *Shaman: The Wounded Healer.* Thames and Hudson, 1982

Harner, Michael. *The Way of the Shaman.* San Francisco: Harper & Row, 1980

Hesse, Hermann. *Narcissus and Goldmund.* Farrar, Straus & Giroux, Inc. 1968

Johnson, Robert A. *Inner Work.* San Francisco: Harper Row, 1986

Kavanaugh, James. *There Are Men Too Gentle To Live Among Wolves.* E,P. Dutton, 1972

Kazantzakis, Nikos. *Report to Greco.* New York: Simon & Shuster, 1965
   Zorba the Greek. New York: Ballantine Books, 1952

Laszlo, Ervin. *Science and the Re-enchantment of the Cosmos: The Rise of the Integral Vision of Reality.* Vermont: Inner Traditions, 2006
   The Akashic Experience: Science and the Cosmic Memory Field. Inner Traditions, 2009

Leonard, George. *The Silent Pulse.* Bantan Books, 1981

Lovelock, James. *Gaia: A New Look at Life on Earth.* Oxford University Press, 1979

Masters, Robert. *The Goddess Sekhmet.* St. Paul: Llewellyn Publications, 1991

Mini, John. *The Aztec Virgin.* Trans-Hyperborean Institute of Science, CA 2000

Moody, Raymond. *Reflections on Life After Death.* Bantam Books, 1978

Murphy, Dan. *Salinas Pueblo Missions.* Tucson: Southwest Parks & Monuments, Assoc. 1994

Pearson, Carol. *The Hero Within: Six Archetypes We Live By.* San Francisco: Harper & Row, 1986

Pernoud, Regine. *Joan of Arc.* New York: Scarborough House, 1994

Pernoud, Regine: Clin, Marie-Veronique. *Joan of Arc: Her Story.* St. Martin's Press, 1998

Picknett, Lynn. *Mary Magdalene.* New York: Carrole & Graf Publishers, 2003

Rimpoche, Sogyol. *The Tibetan Book of Living and Dying.* San Francisco: Harper, 1993 (see pages 306-7 for Purification of the Six Realms)

Sanford, John A. *Dreams: God's Forgotten Language.* New York: Crossroad Publishing, 1989

Shapiro, Francine. *Eye Movement Desensitization and Reprocessing.* New York: The Guilford Press, 2001

Starbird, Margaret. *The Woman with the Alabaster Jar.* Santa Fe: Bear & Co., 1993

Stone, Merlin. *When God Was a Woman.* Harcourt Brace Jovanovich, 1976

Tourin, Christine. *Illuminations: Labyrinthian Music* (CD). Emerald Harp Productions, 2000

Van der Post, Laurens. *Mantis Carol.* Island Press, 1975

Verny, Thomas MD. *The Secret Life of the Unborn Child.* Park Ridge, NJ: The Parthenon Publishing Group, 1988

Vietnam Memorial Directory of Names. Washington D.C.: Vietnam Veterans Memorial Fund, 1991

Walker, Barbara. *The Crone: Woman of Age, Wisdom and Power.* San Francisco: Harper & Row, 1985

Webb, James. *Born Fighting.* Broadway Books, 2004

Wesselman, Hank. *Visionseeker: Shared Wisdom from the Place of Refuge.* Carlsbad, CA: Hay House, 2001

Williams, Margery. *The Velveteen Rabbit.* Running Press, 1981

RESOURCES

Center for Grief and Traumatic Loss, LLC Libertyville, Illinois founded by Allan Botkin for Induced After Death Communication Therapy and Training. Web site: www.inducedadc.com. 847-680-0279

Divine Feminine and Awakened Masculine Institute. P O Box 948 Haiku, HI 96708 Email: infor@divine-feminine.com. Web site: www.divine-feminine.com. 877-731-7500

EMDR Institute. Training or referrals. Email: inst@emdr.com Web site: www.emdr.comP.O. Box 750, Watsonville, CA 95077. 831-372-3900

Foundation for Shamanic Studies founded by Michael Harner. Offers Basic Workshop of Core Shamanism (prerequisite for advanced work) PO Box 1939, Mill Valley, CA 94942. Email: Info@shamanism.org. Web site: www.shamanism.org. 415-897-4583

International Harp Therapy Program founded by Christine Tourin. Training and practitioners. P O Box 333 Mt. Laguna, CA 91948. Email: Harprealm@aol.com. Web site: www.harprealm.com 619-473-0008

Shared Wisdom offers Shamanic Training Workshops and Seminars by Hank Wesselman. E-mail: hank@sharedwisdom.com. Web site: www.sharedwisdom.com

Silvereign Workshops & Consultations. Jody Rowe Staley, Psychic, Spiritual Counselor 1333 N.E. 100th St. Miami Shores, Fl 33138 jrstaley@bellsouth.net 305-757-8994

NOTE FROM THE AUTHOR

I believe every person has a legacy handed down from their ancestors and a destiny in this lifetime. Over the years my life has been filled with many opportunities and challenges that crossed my path. Learning from them continues to be my lesson; sharing some of these adventures is my privilege. They are not meant to be a "how to" or advice, but an acknowledgment that we are all spirits having a human experience. Welcome to the club.

I am no longer available to the public to offer counseling, therapy, dreamwork or psychopomp services. Although the book—*Thea Spiritual Midwife*—tells many stories of cleansing, healing, and guiding souls, these are my personal experiences. I am not responsible for the results of anyone else using these practices. The Bibliography and Resources can act as a guide to find further information, inspiration and/or practitioners.

My memoir is meant to offer a message of hope about life before and after death. The rituals and ceremonies in the book are practices I've discovered along the way. Remember all rituals and ceremonies are to be performed with honor, respect and prayerful intent. Before using any ritual call in your spiritual helpers for guidance; if you are offering the ritual for another, call in their spiritual helpers as well. Cleanse your own negative emotions before beginning and offer a prayer of gratitude at the conclusion.

Many blessings and safely home friends!

ABOUT THE AUTHOR

Jacqueline Thea, PhD, MFT.

 Licensed Psychotherapist, Guardian/Conservator, former Registered Nurse, Dream Counselor, Practitioner of Harp Therapy, trained in Shamanic Studies and After Death Communication.

Thea has spent more than 35 years researching, writing, speaking, living and traveling on sacred quest in California, Colorado, New Mexico, Hawaii, Micronesia, Mexico, Greece, Egypt and France. She now lives in Oregon with her three cats.

APPENDIX I

Eight Basic Agreements About The Afterlife
From Three Ancient Spiritual Traditions

During her travels, experiences and studies, Jacqueline Thea found time-honored wisdom that could be synthesized to enrich our current culture's understanding of life and death. She discovered from the ancient spiritual traditions of Shamanism, Egyptian Mythology and Tibetan Buddhism a core of eight basic agreements.

1. *Every human being has a living soul that survives death.*

2. *The soul is divine and after death desires to return home.*

3. *The soul is part of a Divine Life Force.*

4. *Light is a symbol and direct experience of the Divine Life Force.*

5. *Judgment or life review exists after death.*

6. *Both friendly and unfriendly forces exist in the afterlife.*

7. *Restless souls can be stuck between worlds and unable to move on.*

8. *The living can help the dead.*

The last basic agreement—*the living can help the dead*—provides a foundation for contemporary spiritual midwifery. Although every person and every death is unique, the journey is similar enough to create guidelines so that people who so choose, with loving concern and prayers, can help a departed soul move on to the light and return home.

And, those of us who are now living can enhance our lives by using practices such as clearing our negative emotions, healing our attachments and addictions, or using music and meditation to find peace within and face death without fear.

APPENDIX II

CLEANSING OF NEGATIVE EMOTIONS

Negative emotions can accumulate at particular psycho-physical energy centers in the body, also known as chakras. Negative emotions and/or addictions can keep a lost soul trapped between worlds, needing help. Thea found a visualization and meditation ritual to purify the body of the six main negative emotions from *The Tibetan Book of Living and Dying* (pp.306-7) by Sogyal Rinpoche. The emotion of anger is believed to be located at the soles of the feet. Avarice or greed rests at the base of the trunk, ignorance at the navel. Doubt rests at the heart, jealousy at the throat, and pride rests at the crown of the head. Thea also learned that sound and music are effective and simple means to clear and restore balance to an individual's energy system. She accompanied the ritual with harmonic chords on the harp.

The cleansing can be done with or without the harmonics and can be used to help the living as well as the dead. When Thea uses this ritual—or any ritual—she calls in her spiritual helpers and guardian angels for guidance and support. Then she first cleanses her own negative emotions before offering herself as a channel for healing others. When ready, she envisions the troubled soul she wishes to help and imagines light from above flowing through that body down to the soles of the feet and *sees* all the karma (self-created destiny) created by anger dissolving into the light. Next, moving to the base of the trunk, she images all the karma created by greed dissolving into the light. Continuing with the same procedure at each realm—ignorance at the navel, doubt at the heart, jealously at the throat and pride at the crown of the head—Thea sees the negative patterns dissolving into the healing light. At the end of the practice, Thea *sees* the entire person with her mind's eye surrounded in that radiant light and ends the ritual with a prayer: *May the Mother Light shine upon you. May all love and compassion surround you and may the Child Light within you, guide you safely home.*

APPENDIX III

Ceremonial Release Of The Soul Six Weeks After Death

Several spiritual traditions embrace the belief that a departed soul can linger up to six weeks in this physical realm completing unfinished business. Thea actively honors and remembers departed souls for that period and created this personal ritual for her husband.

Mitch died on March 20, 2009—the first day of spring. Six weeks later on May Day, the time had arrived to honor his soul and bid him farewell. Inside their home, everything had been left in its place since the day Mitch suffered his stroke (two weeks before his death), just in case his spirit happened by. Su, the minister of healing who officiated at Mitch's memorial service, came to the house for this ceremonial release of his soul.

As a practice, Mitch performed a house blessing whenever he moved into a new home using holy water from the Greek Church. He touched and blessed every opening—doors, windows, fireplaces and vents—to clear away old energy and keep negative spirits from entering.

In remembrance of Mitch, Thea provided Su with water she deemed "holy" and asked her to bless all the openings in the home—inside and out. Su also blessed the chairs where Mitch sat, the bed where he slept and the clothes that he wore. She honored his soul, freeing him to come and go as he chose. Thea read a poem and other tributes received from friends and loved ones—cards of sympathy and blessings, and played appropriate music. After closing the ceremony with prayer, old props no longer needed were cleared away—the walker, pillows, breathing machines and medicine. "Safely Home!" Thea whispered to her beloved husband and then celebrated the ceremony at their favorite restaurant with an appropriate toast.